Cultivating Religious
Growth Groups

The Pastor's Handbooks

Cultivating Religious Growth Groups

Charles M. Olsen

The Westminster Press
Philadelphia

First edition

Published by The Westminster Press ®
Philadelphia, Pennsylvania

PRINTED IN THE UNITED STATES OF AMERICA

9 8 7 6 5 4 3 2 1

Library of Congress Cataloging in Publication Data

Olsen, Charles M., 1935–
    Cultivating religious growth groups.

    (The Pastor's handbooks)
    Includes index.
    1. Church group work. 2. Pastoral theology. I. Title.
II. Series.
BV652.2.O42 1984   254   83-27328
ISBN 0-664-24617-6 (pbk.)

I thankfully dedicate this book to all who have enabled me to experience "community" and reflect on its meaning and significance—to my family, congregation, small groups, and base communities in which I have been nurtured. I am especially appreciative of a network of small-group enablers around the world with whom I have tasted and shared life.

Contents

Cultivating Religious
Growth Groups

Introduction

The Pastor as Manager

Let me paint a picture for you. And let me invite you, Pastor, to step into the middle of this picture.

The picture is one of your congregation as fully alive! Your offices are bound together, giving direction to the church's life and ministry. They model Christian community with their energy, spirit, and care. Significant numbers of your laypeople share community in small groups. They are growing in their faith, becoming biblically and theologically aware. They are taking steps into outreach, expressing their "callings" and lay ministries both individually and through the groups in which they participate. Few of the groups look alike. Yet they experience the common dynamics of forming, growing, learning, and terminating. The groups are not "divisive," for your church leadership sees them as a primary vehicle through which the life and ministry of the congregation are expressed. The small groups are endorsed and blessed in the congregation's corporate worship services, the church budget, the planning process, and by you, the pastor.

Step into the picture. No, you will not be on the sidelines with your hands folded, hoping and praying that the picture will be realized and that everything will turn out right. No, you will not be the worn-out leader of every group. Yes, you will be in the center of the picture functioning as a *manager* of the life and mission of the congregation through small groups.

The manager in the picture is not an autocratic overlord. Neither is he or she a sneaky manipulator of people. The manager is a positive rather than a negative person in the picture. Catch a glimpse of an exciting and creative pastoral role—as manager of ministry through groups.

You may say: "That's not me. I could never do that. I can't see myself in your picture." Friend, never say never! I think you *can* do it. I know from experience that pastors can function in managerial roles. As director of Project Base Church, I personally led a series of training sessions on small-group leadership over a three-year period. We predicted that most of our trainees would be laypersons from para church house groups or from congregations. Instead, over 90 percent of the participants were pastors right out of congregations like yours who wanted to learn how they could develop congregational life through small groups.

You may be suspicious of small groups. You may fear small groups. You may be intimidated by small groups. You may feel inadequate around small groups. But no matter what your experience level may have been, or what your feelings are toward small groups, I want to work with you—to start right where you are and lead you step by step into the middle of the picture as a skilled, sensitive, and effective manager.

We will touch your experience of intimate community, whether it has been in family, athletics, business, a vocation, or education. We will use that experience as a bridge to the intentional Christian community of the small group.

We will take your training and education, even though it may have been in a highly directive "answer-giving" style, and expand and adapt it into an enabling-process leadership style that is able to assimilate the initiative and gifts of your lay parishioners.

We will affirm your theology and find ways to weave it into an ongoing story of pilgrimage in a faith journey. Your people can make theological discoveries and affirmations as they travel.

Of Small Groups. Small groups in the church are certainly not new. Jesus gathered a small group of twelve persons with whom he shared his life, feelings, and wisdom. The church that exploded into the Roman world met in small house assemblies. The monastic movement gathered men and women into intentional communities with fixed covenants and responsibilities. Renewal and revival movements have grown through the yeast and leaven of small groups. The Wesleyan and charismatic movements are two notable examples. In fact, congregations already have small groups—committees, choirs, church school classes, and special organizations. So small groups are not new.

But what *is* new is the deliberate attempt to utilize their full potential as vehicles of congregational life, program, and mission.

By small, I am thinking of an ideal range of seven to fifteen persons. Here each participant can be known by name and face. Intimate relationships of trust and sharing can be built. The outside range for a group is from three to thirty-five persons. I know some very effective three-person groups. We have also learned from attempts to build "style-centered" congregations that these congregations cease to grow when they reach thirty-five persons. If the congregations change their style and begin to subgroup, the groups may grow. But maintaining the "Let's all decide and participate together" motto will fix a maximum number who can, in effect, seal off the group from further potential growth.

When saying "small group," I do not have a fixed stereotype group in mind. I do not necessarily visualize the typical prayer group of ten persons who always follow a prayer format. I do not necessarily see a study group gathered on Sunday mornings around a specified curriculum. No. Instead, I see a broad and rich variety of small groups that bear all the basic marks of the church (worship, fellowship, nurture, mission). These are not "anything goes" groups but rather groups that have both an identity as "church" and intentionality which grows out of participation in Christian community.

In Congregations. The limits of our inquiry also place small groups within congregations. To be sure, there has been much vitality over the last twenty years in the small-group movement. Para church organizations have reinforced the movement and many laypersons have gained firsthand experience of the ecumenical church. The limitations, however, inherent in group death, schism, heresy, and manipulation must be weighed against the vitality of these groups outside regular congregations. That is not to say that groups in congregations are less vulnerable to problems, but an accountability does exist in congregations, which fosters health. Therefore the focus of our discussion will place small groups in congregational settings.

Fundamental to our strategy projections for the church are the convictions that life exists in the cellular group, that small groups have a limited life cycle, and that living groups must function within some larger connectional framework. These basic principles will chart the course for congregational development.

The Approach of This Handbook

This book is intended to be a practical handbook. As such, it should be a useful tool primarily to pastors but also to lay leaders who are charged with the tasks of enabling and managing the program of the church. Each chapter will attempt to touch several aspects that will assist the pastor in managing healthy groups. They are:

1. To provide understanding about small-group theory. The learnings from the behavioral sciences, the small-group and house church movements, and organizational development efforts over the last fifteen years provide the church with invaluable data on which to build. We will examine that theory within the various developmental stages of the life cycle of a group.

2. To see groups in a theological framework. Our biblical and theological traditions can inform both the why and the how of group process. Rather than assuming that theological connec-

tions are being made, each chapter will touch these bases.

3. To assist you as pastor to define your unique role as a manager of ministry in the congregation.

4. To enable leadership skill development for both clergy and lay leaders of groups. Groups are never leaderless, so the leaders should be as skilled and aware as they can be.

5. To build congregational life. The church is a system with communication patterns, power lines, decision-making processes, and a corporate "soul." Our attempts to build congregations through groups will need to pay attention to the total system. Healthy congregations will not develop if groups are added on the top of its structure, but only if they develop within the structure.

I

Managerial Roles of the Pastor

Wheat and tares together sown
Unto joy or sorrow grown.

The surge of fashionableness of the small-group movement is over in America. Gone are the days when significant numbers of laypeople just got together in small groups. Gone are the days when para church renewal conferences worshiped and held high the banner of small groups as a cure-all for spiritual apathy or a quick fix for congregational renewal. In the late 1960s and early 1970s small groups proliferated. They sprang up without pastoral initiative or church organization. They were reinforced by lay conferences, by sensitivity and encounter group efforts in business and education, and by an avalanche of supportive books and materials.

Small groups are still present on the church scene today. But there is a difference. Instead of raging like forest fires that leap and move over the terrain with a quick burn of ashes and destruction, small groups are being carefully built like small bonfires around which people gather for warmth or to forge mission. They are carefully nurtured and maintained for ongoing ministry. And pastors are tending the fires.

In a recent effort to update some research on small groups through the Alban Institute, I studied twenty-five congregations that had small groups within them. My objective was to identify and study certain common factors. The most dominant factor was the involvement of pastors in an ongoing effort to build and maintain small groups. Their work was not toward a quick "flash in the pan," "here today, gone tomorrow" program, but toward an ongoing, year after year system of group building. Group life in the congregations could not have been maintained without the full commitment and active involvement of the pastors, as well as the support of lay leaders. The pastors were active managers and, as such, functioned within the following roles:

1. The Planter
Jesus provides us with a picture of the agricultural methods of his day when he tells how "a sower went forth to sow." The seed was scattered about, to find rest upon hard paths, rocky, thin soils, and weed-infested areas or upon good, fallow soils. The farmer knew that only a portion of the seed would actually yield a harvest.

Today's modern farmer is much more selective in planting seeds. Only well-prepared soils are used. Expensive computer-controlled planters place the seeds at proper depth and space. Herbicides and insecticides provide protection for the young growing plants. Seeds have been carefully selected to thrive within the limits of the growing season and climate conditions.

These agricultural-oriented contrasts of seed planting may be compared to the planting of small groups. In the past, pastors recognized the potential for life in the sprouting seeds of newly forming small groups. But they also despaired at the effort expended to scatter seeds that never germinated. These pastors became puzzled at the way vibrant, growing groups could wither away. They became dismayed at how conflicts, digressions, and pettiness could choke off life. Often people just hoped that groups would form spontaneously while at the same time fearing how they would handle them if they did "get going." I remember the unenthusiastic witness of a pastor who said: "Small groups? Yes. We tried them once. We had five or six vital groups going. Then they sort of fizzled out. We tried them and found they don't work."

Rather than planting by wish, trial and error, or blind hope, you and others can now plant groups in a selective, intentional manner. The church in recent years has come to see itself as a "system" in its communication patterns, planning and evaluation efforts, and attempts at conflict resolution. This voluntary organization consists of a whole network of people and groups whose growth, calls, and commitments are "managed" and enabled.

These are years of institution building. No one needs to be a dummy anymore about small groups. You the pastor can profit from the learnings from the house church movement, human relations disciplines, and the new understandings about the church's own structure. From these learnings you can work to develop the life of a congregation through a variety of small groups. And that is exactly what many churches are doing.

Of all the occupations in which people have historically engaged, the farmer above all has established the reputation for hard work. His work is never done. He works the fields from sunrise to sunset. He "makes hay while the sun shines." He lives close to the land and to his livestock.

As a pastor who manages groups, you will work hard. You will develop clear priorities, being willing to lay aside some activities for which the congregation has varying expectations. The investment of time and emotion is real.

Hal Edwards, who works with pastors and churches through Christian Laity of Chicago, observes that there is a price to pay:

> I see our particular movement becoming more local church connected, especially over the last three years. For example, we have developed very healthy relationships with a few clergy and we see the quality of small groups and the network of small groups quietly solidifying as we cross-fertilize each other in the local churches through CLC ministries. I see small groups today not as a fad or something people ought to join, so much as an

opportunity for those people who are aware and ready to initiate and "pay the price" for longevity and gradual growth together. (Hal Edwards, personal correspondence, 1981. Used by permission)

Job descriptions and annual professional goal statements must reflect the investment. An intensive group program cannot be a hobby that runs over and above energies. To choose to invest in groups is a choice to reduce some other aspects of normal congregational ministry.

The First Presbyterian Church of Arlington Heights, Illinois, wrote a job description and secured a staff member with orientation toward small groups.

The pastor of the Immanuel of the Hill Episcopal Church in Alexandria teaches five weekly two-hour-long theology groups in a four-year program—and thinks it is worth the investment. The participants must be freed from other church activities in order to participate.

The senior rector of Truro Parish of Fairfax, Virginia, gives primary attention to preaching and teaching, oversight of groups, and leading the lay shepherds of groups. Other staff persons care for other ministries.

The harvest becomes the payoff for the hardworking farmer and planter. The production of good grain, rather than chaff or weeds, provides a deep-seated satisfaction and fulfillment of one's calling and vocation.

2. *The Prophet*

One of the promises at Pentecost was that the Holy Spirit would enable young and old alike to dream and envision the possible future. The pastor as prophet "sees" the big picture and holds that picture for the future. The vision is for a strong congregation that is built on the strength of a variety of cellular small groups.

Most pastors have had some positive experience of a supportive, caring community. Many have become acquainted with small-group process in conferences, clinical pastoral training, mission/action groups, seminary teams, or clergy support groups. Let those experiences become the starting point in creating your own vision. If the process of envisioning is really one of projecting your values into a new or future setting, then identify those aspects of community (such as inclusion, affirmation, trust, participation, and responsibility) that can fill out the picture. See the whole with its related parts.

Imagine, for instance, that your congregation is like a cathedral, which consists of a group of parishes interacting with each other through the cathedral.

Try the following procedure for envisioning, which has been developed for organizations. Draw a skeleton picture of two churches, side by side. Label one "Is" and the other "To Be." Within "Is," place a series of plus and minus signs, labeling what each stands for. Within "To Be," mark as plus that which you would like to carry over from "Is" to "To Be," drawing a connecting line between the two. Then connect some pluses in "To Be" with some minuses in "Is," drawing connecting lines from minus to plus, identifying how a *change* could be made to convert the minus to plus. In addition, mark some pluses in "To Be" that would be brand new. Thus the new vision of "To Be" would consist of (1) pluses carried over from "Is," (2) pluses that are converted negatives from "Is," and (3) some new pluses that are added. If the vision is to create a church with caring community, or biblical and theological awareness, or active lay ministries, you can see how pluses and minuses can be identified relative to small groups in the big picture.

You the pastor will not only engage in and enable the envisioning process for lay leaders but will become an interpreter of the process for the congregation. Invite churches that have small-group programs to tell their stories. Looking into case studies is an excellent way to begin to shape a vision. Change can take place if people are aware of other possible options for them. A peek inside other churches that work through small groups can open wide vistas.

Remember, where there is no vision, the people perish! Thus spoke the prophet. And you are a prophet of vision!

3. *The Cultivator*

Groups are cultivated, not made. Proper chemistry, time for gathering, and a spark of life all combine to make a group more than the sum of its parts. Then the gift of community lies before the cultivator, who played an indispensable role in bringing new life into being, yet confesses that a miracle happened before one's very eyes.

The pastor as cultivator plays an active role in initiating new groups in the congregation. An overall effort is made to communicate what small groups do and are for—through preaching, newsletters, and lay stories. Working with the official board, the pastor can offer various opportunities for people to enter the groups. Five of the most commonly used "entry doors" are:

a. *New Member Classes*
Example:

The First Presbyterian Church of Bethlehem, Pennsylvania, conducts a six-week Inquirers Class. At the conclusion of this class, the members are invited to continue for six additional weeks, during which time they go farther into the experience of community. Both series are led by a staff pastor. Then the new members are invited to continue as an ongoing group under lay leadership.

b. *Exploration Groups*
Examples:

The La Salle Street Church of Chicago, Illinois, works at developing new groups in geographical neighborhoods. A lay "catalyst" leader assists them for eight weeks; then they are on their own, with periodic support.

The West Hills Presbyterian Church of Omaha, Nebraska, provides a trained clergy or lay leader for a new group for a period of four weeks. The leader then assists the group to draw up a covenant under which they will operate for thirteen weeks.

The pastor of the Hope Lutheran Church of Clinton, Virginia, personally works with a group for nine months in a "Discovery of Ministry" group. He then introduces them to the five basic marks of small-group and church life. The group elects its own leader(s) and, after a summer of informal activities, begins in earnest by September to function around those five marks (worship, fellowship, nurture, witness, service).

c. *The Beginning (September) of the Program Year*

Most churches put a heavy interpretive and invitational blitz on the congregation early in September. These new groups function for nine months, then ease off for the summer. They would either terminate or contract again for each additional year in the following fall.

Examples:

Trinity Presbyterian Church of Harrisonburg, Virginia, has built its life around mission house churches since its inception as a new congregation over fifteen years ago. At the conclusion of an annual fall retreat, opportunity is given to call new groups into being or renew the call for an existing group. Each call is related to a mission cause.

The Parkway Christian Church of Plantation, Florida, has worked at group development for sixteen years. After several weeks of emphasis through the newsletter and lay presentations, people are invited to sign cards and bring them forward on a September "Commitment Sunday" worship service to participate in a basic "K" group or a choice of other groups.

The Whittier Area Baptist Fellowship of Whittier, California, experimented with various ways of placing people in groups. They were finally led to develop and offer a series of group contracts that people could buy into. Two lead couples (plus others) develop a covenant around specific areas of need or interest and indicate the number of openings that exist. At the end of the summer all contracts are mailed to the congregation in preparation for a two-week sign-up period. Each fall new groups are started, although some previous groups may be getting back together.

d. *The Vision and Call of Members*

We have already seen the "calling" aspect of group invitation in the program year. Many churches that open the door to seasonal calling also incorporate a process whereby calls may be issued at any time in response to a given situation.

Example:

The Church of the Saviour of Washington, D.C., has built mission groups and mission congregations upon the calls of its laypersons. One or more persons, after much prayer and searching, can "sound the call," which becomes the central "outward journey" focus of a new group. Specific strategies can come later in the group's life.

e. *The Particular Needs of People*

Given the high mobility within society in general, and the lack of "community" within our large urban areas, a primary human need seems to be for a place to belong, to grow, and to express one's gifts.

Recent studies have shown that people are most open to the church when they have experienced change in their lives.

The Grubb Institute in London suggests that people oscillate between autonomous and dependency modes of existence. At particular times of change or crisis, they especially need to lean on the church community.

4. *The Physician*

Small groups follow a life cycle, as do the seasons or our physical bodies. The training design of this handbook is constructed on the developmental stages. But few pastors are aware of the lifeline of groups. Those who work at it year after year begin to pick up some repeating dynamics.

Examples:

St. Mark's Episcopal Church of Washington, D.C., follows a basic educational process in all its groups—new members, task, and growth. There are five stages: curiosity, anxiety, resolution, despair, and anticipation. These stages are tied to the group dependence, independence, and interdependence relationships with the leaders. The stages are also interpreted by the seasons of the church year.

The New Providence (New Jersey) Presbyterian Church observes three phases of development: enchantment, disenchantment, and deep love. They train group leaders for two months in recognition of these phases, as well as in aspects of group death.

A good physician is intimately acquainted with the stages of physiological development and deterioration. The doctor is conversant with birth, coordination, adolescence, vital signs, injury, trauma, disease, infection, health, decay, and death. With this knowledge, he or she will treat the patient within the life stage and situation that is observed.

Would you allow a doctor who was unschooled, blind, or insensitive to the developmental rhythms of life to treat you or your children? Probably not, you say. It would be unthinkable.

So the pastor who manages groups will be a good physician who can recognize the signs of the times. This role is crucial, and we will examine it at considerable depth.

5. *The Coach*

In rare instances you might as pastor be the ongoing leader of a small group. (Moderating the regular meetings of an official board is the most notable exception to the rarity of leading groups directly.) You as pastor cannot be present at every group gathering—nor should you be. So your managing role will need to take place from some distance.

Small groups are never leaderless. Roles as leaders always emerge, even if at times they are shared by several persons in the group. A trust in lay leadership will have to be cultivated. Some pastors with high control needs may find this difficult at first, but such trust can be developed. I am not calling for removal of the pastor from the small-group scene, but rather for functioning in a supportive capacity.

The successful coach will be effective if he or she is proficient in three tasks: *(a)* Player selection and placement. The right talent at the right position will build a strong team. *(b)* Training and skill development. Long hours on the practice field before the game will ensure that the athletes are ready to give their best to the game. *(c)* Sideline support and direction. The heat of battle tests the ability of a coach to adjust to the game situation, carry out strategies, and provide the emotional support that is needed for the players to persist until the job is finished.

The selection of group leaders takes place in a variety of ways. Look for the natural leaders. They may have already demonstrated leadership in other church functions. Look for persons who have shown leadership outside the church but have never found their niche in the congregation. Look for persons who are giving evidence of making positive changes in their lives—who are growing spiritually and emotionally. Look for persons who are genuine in expressing their feelings—who can laugh and cry. Look for those whom people trust. If a group is selecting its own leader, let the members identify the person(s) they trust most. Finally, look for persons who click with others and who have the capacity to act on hunch and intuition.

You as pastor may not be the sole or primary selector, but you will have an important role to play.

Pregame training is best conducted in a seminar setting. You will have the opportunity to "model" the training you are giving. The material in this handbook on the skills that are called for to enable a group at each stage of its life would provide an excellent resource. The experience of the seminar group in its own developmental stages can be used for reflection and learning. I have found that practice in the training group itself can be beneficial. Invite one of the group to lead in making a decision, to guide the group in shared prayers or in role playing.

Perhaps it is impossible ever fully to train and equip a person to lead a group before the fact. Simultaneous sideline coaching may be the most effective. Here you as pastor can meet regularly with your group leaders. Let them report together (without violating confidences) what is happening in the groups, how they have tried to lead, and how they feel about their roles. Your lay leaders will learn from each other, from your ongoing training, and from their own experience. In addition, they will have a place in a support group for which they are not ultimately responsible.

Example:
The ten groups of the Winnetka (Illinois) Presbyterian Church meet every other week. A core group, consisting of one representative from each of the Koinonia groups, meets monthly. This core group is the Spiritual Life Committee of the session. Instead of the groups being autonomous entities, they are now within the intentional ministry of the church. The church is in a position to be supportive of them.

6. *The Scout*
You get a lot of resources through the mail. You never ordered most of them. Sometimes you may feel that the church is going to die of its own paper weight. You receive brochures on training conferences, catalogs for books and materials, samples of study guides, reports of commissions and task groups, and so on. You walk through a good bookstore and are overwhelmed by the volume of really worthwhile material.

So you may be surprised when your lay leaders of small groups wonder if there is anything available that might help their group. You are the best scout and selection committee the church has. You are in a unique position with unique discernment to judge the quality and usefulness of materials that are available. Groups will ask you for good resources that they can use. They have reason to expect that you can respond positively.

In addition to your own files or bookshelf, see that your church library grows a section of helps for groups with books, tapes, and video materials. Integral to this effort is establishing a budget for the support of small groups. Money may be requested for resources or to aid special projects in which the group is involved.

You also know people who would enrich the life of a group if they were invited for an evening of "conversation."

People, money, and materials are all part of a resourcing system in which you will be involved. You are perched on "lookout"!

7. *The Consultant*

Most church groups of which I am aware hold an open-door policy toward the pastor. We pastors have a standing invitation to "drop in anytime." When I do that I often find that they want to tell me about their life together—where the good places are and where the dry and hard places are. I move very quickly into an intervening consultant role.

The consultant role is a legitimate one. Often the group gets stuck and an intervention is appropriate and welcomed.

Goal setting, planning, and covenanting are some of the occasions when a pastor is invited to share in the process. I know of one pastor who attends each group quarterly when the members set their goals. He is then also able to ask, "How did you do on the goals you set when we last met three months ago?"

Conflict resolution may be too difficult for a regular leader to handle, especially if he or she is a party in the conflict. As a pastoral consultant, you can help group members share their feelings, establish communication, forgive a wrong, explore options, and make new decisions. Increasing resources and training conferences in conflict resolution focused on the congregation are now available for pastors. The training is certainly applicable to small groups.

Later in this handbook we will examine the dynamics of group termination. A trusted consultant who can help a group evaluate its life "in the valley of the shadow of death" is a real shepherd. At that point an outsider with good skills provides a service that could not be found within the group, given its emotional charge.

Or the group may have something to celebrate. Your participation affirms the members' joy. A birth, new home, marriage, completion of a study or task, or victory in a mission goal calls for a party. Jesus would have been there. Why shouldn't we? "Rejoice with those who rejoice!"

8. *The Theologian*
You as pastor are normally the most qualified and best trained person in the congregation to serve as theologian for the church as a whole. By that I do not mean that the pastor is the answer person. Pastors often tend to fall into that trap, thereby shortchanging the small groups from the adventure of theological discovery.

As theologian, you the pastor are a "bearer of tradition." You bring the stories of faith, the richness of the biblical witness, or the history of the church into a present setting. That role can be expressed in training lay leaders but is most vital in the ongoing preaching ministry. Your sermons are the most visible context where theologizing about "community" can take place, giving the whole congregation, as well as small-group participants, understanding from a biblical and theological framework. You will help them make sense out of their experience.

As theologian, you the pastor also should be skilled in the process of enabling laypersons in small groups to theologize. By that I mean to connect their real-life experience with the biblical story, while looking for meanings, values, and faith affirmations. One section of this book will go into detail about that skill.

9. *The Leader of Worship*
Where does liturgy, work and worship, come into play for people in small groups? Often we reserve worship for the sanctuary. Yet many small groups are discovering the place of worship in their own setting, including the conduct of Sacraments. The pastor will not lead worship in every small group, yet can assist them in the use of simple worship structures and can help them make connections with corporate worship in the larger congregation. The pastor will be needed to conduct Communion services.

At times the pastor may be invited into a group to conduct

absolution—to lead people to forgive each other. Often when a group terminates, a funeral service needs a pastor to assist in saying good-by, releasing the memories and hopes to God.

10. *The Spiritual Guide*

The small groups of the 1960s and early 1970s tended to build community by interpersonal relations. Self-disclosure, interaction, confrontation, and affirmation were used to bring people together.

In recent years some of the age-old methods of Christian spiritual discipline—silence, prayer, meditation, and guided imagery—have been imported into small groups. These groups practice together what once was reserved for private experience. And they are discovering a closeness, unity, and intimacy that can only be explained as gift. The object is spiritually to "let go" or "surrender to the Lord."

You as pastor and spiritual guide will play an active role in permitting and enabling people to offer themselves to God. Yes, there you really do stand on holy ground—in the mystery of God's touch of human life at its deepest levels.

2

Life Cycle—
The Crucial Key

> For everything there is a season. . . .
> A time for birth and a time for death
> A time for planting and a time for pulling up . . .
> A time for building and a time for tearing down.
>   Ecclesiastes 3:1–3

You the pastor who cultivates groups in churches will, like the wise farmer, be intimately acquainted with the seasons. Planting, growth, and harvest become inbred into one's psyche, habits, intuitions, thinking, and work. You the pastor will know and have a feel for the life cycle of small groups, which is the crucial key for their cultivation.

Group Theory

The laws of nature and the changing of seasons reveal the fundamental principles of existence. Plant and animal life go through the cycles of birth, development, functioning, and death. The fruit produces seed, which repeats the cycle. Life is in the seed. The structural forms rise, then fall into decay—even becoming food for the new expression of life. Humankind has learned to move with the seasons and reap the rewards of planting, caring, and harvesting.

Social institutions follow the same patterns. Their forms are not permanent. They also rise and fall, come and go.

The life cycle provides a helpful way for pastors and church leaders to look at and understand small groups. Awareness and recognition of the life-cycle phcnomena are a path to freedom. Blindness to or denial of the cycle will ultimately lead to frustration, disillusionment, or guilt. Our world (and even our churches) tends to define success with permanence, survival, stability, and longevity. How we pastors get seduced by these standards! But a new standard is raised for us—a standard of managing and cultivating groups as they move through predictable stages to ultimate termination. We will be able to feel good about our ministry, even when the groups have concluded their existence.

No two groups are exactly alike. Each has its own unique characteristics. Their lifetime may be three weeks, three months, three years, or longer. Or they may periodically go through a death-and-rebirth cycle. But their developmental progress will reveal certain common threads, which we want to sort out, identify, and understand.

The social scientists have given much attention to charting the stages of group formation and development. But the books published in the 1960s and 1970s became strangely silent when they approached group termination, including only several paragraphs of oughts and shoulds. If the purpose of a test group was a task, communication, or growth, the descriptions of the stages stopped when that particular goal was achieved. But I had to ask, "Then what?" The human relations groups were usually test or lab groups set in the time frame of a conference, seminar, or classroom. They were not like church-sponsored, voluntary association groups whose time boundaries were open-ended.

Group termination and the complete cycle of group life have been left for us in the church or in other voluntary groups to study.

Work with all types of small groups reveals four major stages along the developmental life-cycle path, as well as numerous critical factors along the way. The life cycle that will be developed in this handbook might be pictured as a time line that runs from left to right, with the stages labeled as initiation, formation, function, and termination.

The church's history and theology leave the church uniquely prepared to deal with this complete life cycle. The Christian tradition provides rich death and resurrection themes that inform group life. Letting go and surrendering out of conscious intention are integral parts of the Christian's spiritual growth and journey.

Willingness to work with the life cycles of small groups will provide us with further understanding of the nature of the church and will enable the building of healthy and powerful congregations!

Picture the church as a body of cells. If one likens it to one's own physical body, the analogy becomes clear. In appearance you are not much different from how you looked ten years ago. If one had known you then, you could be recognized today. Yet science says that a "new person" is present, that is, one with a collection of new cells. Cells die after six or seven years and are replaced. New cells are constantly being formed and old ones are sloughing off. The one exception is within the central nervous system. In the church as the "body of Christ," Christ is the head, in touch with the many parts of the body through an unchanging nervous system. The bones provide structure for flesh. But the body of the church is constructed upon small, living, cellular groups. These small groups become the locus of life itself.

The Pastor's Enabling Skills

Knowing that the life cycle could lead to despair. "What's the use of trying," one might say, "if the death of small groups is so certain?" But let's claim the insight and live with it. By claiming understanding of the life cycle, we can identify and develop effective skills in leadership in ourselves and our lay leaders. Just as we can only really live when we have come to terms with our own death, so groups can only grow to health when they are in touch with their own limited existence under the guidance of understanding leaders.

The church's inability to face the death of groups continually returns to haunt it. Laypeople become bewildered with group closure. Not being able to see, name, and express grief when a group concludes, they carry their unfinished business with them for years. One pastor reported an attempt he made to start a new series of groups. He invited people who had related their good experiences in previous groups over the years. Yet most sent their regrets, which left him somewhat bewildered. The following study may shed some light on their negative responses.

A group for training clergy that I led had varying experiences with small, intensive faith communities. I asked each member to identify a group in which he or she had previously participated. Each pastor then wrote a dialogue with that former group, letting the conversation come from within each one of them. They discovered that even though they were no longer in the group or that the group had terminated, they were not "finished" with the group. They had not dealt with their exit or the group's death. The unfinished business which they continued to carry with them would block them from entering into a new group.

One pastor observed, "We know how to start plenty of programs in our church, but we don't know how to stop them!" He has plenty of company. One vital key to small-group development within the congregation is to recognize the life-cycle nature of groups and deal openly with the termination process. Group leaders need training to help people disengage from intimacy and to do "grief work" openly and unashamedly.

From 1973 to 1975 I directed Project Base Church, a project funded by the Lilly Foundation aimed at finding and feeding the house church movement. I still remember my "aha" experience. I had just begun an advanced training conference for small-group leaders who had already been through Project Base Church's basic training program. Each participant had drawn a picture of his or her training need or goal. The papers were scattered on the floor within the circle we had formed. Suddenly I saw it! I moved to the drawings and rearranged them into an ordered sequence. Before our eyes lay the *life cycle of a small group,* with its stages all in order! I saw for the first time the key to working with small groups—the realization that a life cycle exists, that even healthy groups are subject to birth, growth, and death. I saw the exciting possibilities for skilled leaders who could support small groups through the various stages of their limited life-span.

The discovery of the life-cycle patterns of the primary basic community opened the door to an emerging training design for small-group leaders. The life-cycle training design proved itself over and over again to be on target with the participants' experience of small-group life. Like not seeing the forest for the trees, it was so simple that it often went unrecognized.

Each training conference opens with a presentation of the various stages and components of the life cycle. Each participant then identifies his or her skills, experiences, previous training, or leadership needs related to those stages or components. The remaining days of the training conferences are filled with a rich interaction of the participants, each having something to offer and each getting something in return. The trainer is present to watch it unfold! By the close of the training event, each participant is able to identify specific areas in which he or she wants to develop additional skills. I covet the same excitement for each pastor who sees lay group leaders come alive and build a bank of useful skills through pastor-led training events.

Most recent training conferences on small-group leadership provide skills in how to get people to "open up" into self-disclosure. Our training design, however, places more and more emphasis on group closure, until the two "ends" of group life are in balance. The leader becomes as skilled in concluding a group as in beginning a group.

Practice in Churches

The clincher for the life-cycle thesis came as Project Base Church monitored the life experience of a wide variety of small groups. Finding and feeding the movement led researchers into a linking communication network. They observed a high mortality rate, especially in groups that were not connected to the larger church or did not function within the framework of a local congregation.

A group of researchers from the University of Kansas School of Religion studied fifteen "liberated churches" in 1971. When they returned in 1973 to follow up their examination, only three of the fifteen were still alive! (*National Catholic Reporter*, March 22, 1974.) Alternative forms of the church fell off rapidly around 1972–1973. They simply fell victim to the life cycle.

The unattached small group, house church, or liberated or underground church may have vitality. Its life is out in the open. Its love, trust, and strength, as well as its conflict, weakness, and frailty, are visible for all to see. But when a house church nears the throes of death, few props and supports are available to keep it going. It has no institutional connections. When it loses its vitality, the handwriting is on the wall for all to see. When the group terminates, its members often drop out of sight or get lost between the cracks.

However, in the groups that are attached to a cluster of other groups or that function within a congregation, the participants still have a place, a holding or catch basin in which to take a breather or to link up with an existing or newly forming group. The congregational structure can provide the "bones" for group connection, birth, and death.

The small groups that follow a life cycle function within the church as a "system." The congregation as a volunteer organization is very complex. People who associate with it bring a particular heritage, distinct needs, current information, and hope. The church is organized with lay leaders and pastoral staff to do its work—to manage its life and mission. Its "product" is the care of people, the worship of God, and service to the world.

Example:

Ecumenikos, a congregation of house churches in the Kansas City area which Anne Lee Kreml served, built group birth and death into their system at four-month structural intervals. She described their experiences:

> This restructuring of house churches on a regular basis has been experienced as threatening. The people involved in house church, who have come to experience community at a depth unknown to them before, fear the loss of that experience as a loss which cannot be retrieved. And it is a loss. But it is also significant that the experience of a new creation of community with a new house church has come to be exceedingly meaningful. With the experience of depth community in one house church, our people express joy at newfound love through particular people. With the experience of depth community found in several successive house churches, our people are experiencing the greater faith in the trustworthiness of the house church process, which leads toward faith in an ultimate creative and loving universe. Thus, this month as we begin our fourth restructuring of house churches, those who a year ago were saying, "I cannot leave this group of people; they are my life," are now saying to newer people, "Ending a house church is hard, but you will find more life waiting in another house church." The house church restructuring thus also becomes a mode of addressing the themes of death, grief, and ongoing life within the experiences of the participants. (Anne Lee Kreml, personal correspondence, 1975. Used by permission)

If the small, primary base group forms, functions, and terminates within this system, the following questions are important: How can the congregation develop its life and ministry through the small-group vehicle? How can the groups that form be enabled and nourished by a sensitive congregation? If groups are "friend" rather than the "enemy," "integral" rather than "supplemental," where are the points in which they intersect with the other processes of church life?

3

The Initiating
Stage

First the blade . . .

Group Theory

Without planting there is no harvest. Without birth there is
no life. The managerial roles of the pastor as planter and cultivator are vital in getting things started!

Groups do not start from scratch. They start from something.
The people who come to them, the institution that spawns them,
and the leadership that gathers them all bring a complex set of
personalities, needs, gifts, histories, and visions. Energy for the
group flows before the group ever comes together for the first
time. The initiation stage brings together various personalities,
needs, gifts, histories, and visions, which together result in an
implicit covenant through interpretation and a "call."

1. *Personalities*

Small groups are primarily interpersonal associations of people. Each person brings a unique and distinct *personality*. A
simplistic categorizing of each potential new member as a "bad
apple" or a "good apple" according to the evaluator's own taste
will not prove helpful. But a deeper understanding of variations
within personalities is needed to integrate and build upon the
strength of each as an aid to launching a new group.

The Christian tradition affirms that each person is a unique creation of God and is to be celebrated as such. One successful group leader said, "Our key to good groups is to celebrate the uniqueness of each person!"

Jesus certainly did not recruit a band of look-alikes as his disciples. Each man he called brought a distinct personality. Peter and John, for instance, illustrate the contrasts of flamboyance and reserve, of vociferousness and introspection, of feeling and thinking. Jesus seemed to appreciate the different flavors and did not try to force the men into a uniform mold.

Recent psychological studies have found ways to distinguish and type various personalities. Among them is the Byers-Briggs Type Indicator (Consulting Psychologists Press, 577 College Avenue, Palo Alto, Calif. 94306), which reveals personal preferences along the lines of four continua: (1) Extroversion/introversion: Some people relate to outside people and things, while others prefer inner ideas. (2) Sensing/intuition: While some like to work with solid facts, others prefer possibilities and relationships. (3) Thinking/feeling: Some people may judge by logic and analysis, while others judge by personal values. (4) Judging/perception: Some like an orderly way of life; others are more comfortable being spontaneous. With these preferences in mind, one can look forward to a rich variety of people who will give texture and flavor to the group. The group experience will not affect change in basic personalities, yet these same personalities will always be affecting the process of the group.

2. Needs

People bring their *needs*. No matter what the group is doing, people will work to get their needs met. Those constant and basic needs are the need to be, to belong, and to have and do.

As whole persons in our *be*-ing, we are each aware of our own uniqueness. "No one else is just like me!" We see ourselves as lovable persons and persons of value and worth. We are somebody! Our many needs have been adequately addressed in the gospel. God's unconditional love for his people provides worth and value to each personality. He frees us to become all that we have been created to be.

We need to *belong*. We are social beings, The church is a community. To be "in" is one thing; to feel supported and cared for is another. Moving into a relationship is at the heart of the covenant experience. In the gift of the church, our social and belonging needs are met. That community lives in a covenant bond with God and each other.

We need to *have and do*, to have a sense of destiny and purpose. To work, play, and aspire toward some purpose larger than ourselves provides the ultimate fulfillment. Our call and destiny provides a work to be in mission on God's behalf in his world.

These needs do not simply exist in a vacuum and will most certainly work their way into the agenda and behavior of a small group. The social scientists have charted people's basic needs. Abraham Maslow's familiar hierarchy of needs presents a pyramid, reading from the bottom up: basic survival, safety, belonging, ego-status, and self-actualization (Abraham H. Maslow, *Motivation and Personality,* 2d ed.; Harper & Row, 1970). William Schutz identifies three interpersonal needs: inclusion, affection, and control. His Firo-B test measures the need to give as well as to receive in each of the three areas (William Schutz, *Joy;* Grove Press, 1967).

3. *Gifts*

People bring their *gifts.* These certainly include natural abilities and trained skills, but much more. Biblical faith affirms the rich variety of gifts that the Holy Spirit bestows upon his people. Many of these gifts lie dormant within the Christian because they have never been "called forth." A number of intensive Christian communities see as one of their vital functions the recognition and calling forth of the gifts of their members.

And the gifts are not just for show or self-edification. Their purpose will be to build up the community and to extend mission beyond the community. Ministry could be described as the application of the gifts of God's people to the needs of a hurting world. Paul's list of the gifts from I Corinthians 12 and Romans 12 reveals their wide range: preaching, teaching, encouragement, administration, healing, inspiration, and so forth. The listings are only suggestive, certainly not exhaustive.

People's gifts will shape the group. They cannot be ignored or buried. The group that is sensitive, appreciative, and curious will most certainly be enriched and empowered.

4. *Histories*

People bring their *histories* and stories to the group. Each person has gone through a number of phases or stages in his or her own life. Each stage has had its own beginning and ending. Each stage has wisdom figures attached to it. Each stage was comprised of gains and losses, fulfillment and disappointment, with all the residual feelings of joy, anger, pain, and guilt. These people will be looking for a safe and trusting place to tell their stories and to find acceptance and affirmation for who they are and where they have been.

At certain times they will have need for special types of groups or be more open to participation in a faith community. A research study conducted by the Synod of Texas, "Why People Join the Presbyterian Church U.S.," revealed that "virtually all of the new members in describing the circumstances under which they first began thinking of joining talk about circumstances that involve some major change in their personal situation—marriage, geographical move, vocational change, illness, death, birth of children, going away from home to college or service. The implication is that at such a time a person is most likely to be open to an invitation to consider church membership" ("Why People Join the Presbyterian Church U.S.," p. 21; Synod of Texas, 1968).

The Grubb Institute in London has been studying what creates an openness to participate in the church. Bruce Reed, the director, observes:

In order to survive, human beings are . . . engaged in the process of fluctuating or oscillating between two frames of mind or modes of experience. One mode is characterized by man feeling weak in the face of difficulties and anxieties from within and without, in which condition he seeks to disengage himself from his normal social and working environment. In the second mode of experience man has a sense of wholeness and power which enables him to engage with some confidence in relations with the world and other people around him. ("The Task of the Church and the Role of Its Members," p. 2; Alban Institute, Mt. St. Alban, Washington, D.C., 1980)

Reed points out that these modes of dependence and autonomy condition one's openness to seeking a place in the church. I would further observe that either mode of experience could dictate the need for a small group. The caring community group model which emphasizes personal growth would attract the dependent mode and the mission/task/action-oriented group would attract the autonomous mode.

5. *Visions*

And, finally, people bring their *visions.* Studies in the dynamics of change reveal that—despite one's awareness of the need for change—unless alternative options can be pictured, change will never be realized.

The Pastor's Enabling Skills

Distinct skills are necessary to support a group during each stage of the cycle. The initiating stage demands an awareness in the pastor or lay leader of what people bring to the group: their personalities, hopes, fears, life experiences, values, gifts, and faith commitments. The capacity to listen is crucial, for the leader who interprets and invites people into a group will want to do so within the prospective member's needs and visions. All too often, prospective members become the victims of information overkill. They hunger for community, which groups can satisfy, but fear the risk of investment. The more they hear about intimacy or involvement, the more hesitant they are to join.

Values clarification skills are also useful in capturing a vision for the group. Here is an example: Subdivide the group into three-person subgroups (triads). One person is asked to share a significant experience of community. A second person, the designated listener, repeats back what was heard. The third person listens to identify values that were implicit or explicit in the story. List all the values on a chalkboard or newsprint in front of the total group. The final step projects these values into the new vision for a group. What would our group look like if these values were incorporated?

Once a vision for a new group becomes clear, the pastor can assist others to interpret it to prospective participants. However, at this point communication can become a difficult business. People will hear the descriptions out of their own contexts, experiences, or impressions. They may have preconceived ideas about groups being ingrown, divisive, elitist, superconfessional, "sensitivity," pious, or far out. Interpreting what the group is *not* becomes just as important as interpreting what it is. Inaccurate myths must be corrected before a clear new image can be communicated.

Overzealous testimony to intimate group experiences or to group behavior and activities may scare a person away. Prospective group members carry both the hunger for and the fear of intimacy.

The *invitation* (call) becomes very specific. "Come join us at a specific time and place in order to. . . ." This invitation becomes the implicit contract under which the group will operate during its formation stage. The invitation may also have an open end, which, in large part, is tied to trust of and dependence upon the leaders. "Let's get together to explore what we might mean and be to each other over the next few months. We can decide the specifics later. In the meantime we can share our own hopes and expectations for the group."

The interpreting and inviting functions can be practiced best in role-play situations. One has to walk in another's shoes as well as learn to articulate the vision. One trainee stated that she had acquired many good skills related to group functioning but had frustrated herself by her inability to gather and initiate a new group. She recognized the importance of skills training, even in the initiating stages.

The wise leader will recognize that the group does not begin when everyone gathers for the first meeting. The group will be loaded with enough "stuff" to either flourish or self-destruct!

Oh, yes, one thing more. Assume that God has been and is at work in each person's life. And count on Christ's promise that where two or three are gathered in his name, he will be present to continue his work through this corporate community of faith!

Practice in Churches

How are new groups initiated in congregations? Just as we have examined what each individual brings to a group and have taken that seriously, so let us now look at what the congregation contributes. Needs and visions provide a starting place for the prospective group members. Likewise, the existing information-gathering, communication, and planning processes of a church can become a launching pad for groups.

How is *information gathered* that will uncover the needs, concerns, and visions for people?

Examples:

A prayer request box or bulletin board

A random survey of the congregation via the mail

The first stage of a planning process

Area or national church concerns that appear in periodicals

Life-planning labs

The *communication systems* of a church can invite people into groups.

Examples:

The weekly printed bulletin

Telephone chains

Regular newsletters

Pastoral letters

Shared presentations by laypersons in worship

Preaching and teaching platforms that interpret Christian community

The *planning process,* as it involves lay members, officers, and clergy, can provide a ripe setting for new groups. As both short-range and long-range goals are set, the next question becomes one of strategy. How can particular small groups in the church accomplish certain specific goals? An annual, ongoing planning process becomes a natural opening for group life!

Church program events, which grow out of the deliberations of the officers or committees, can include a variety of small groups. The advantage of these events lies in the clear "contract" and specifics of how, when, where, and what. They also have fixed time frames in which to operate. Adult elective courses are one prime illustration.

An open "call" procedure leaves room for lay-initiated groups to come together around a concern or a need that may be immediate or grow out of a particular situation. This bottom-up approach to church programming in addition to top-down offerings of clergy and officers takes every church member seriously. The task of the pastor then is to help communicate the call, to assist those who gather around the call to form a group, and to support the group in its explorations and tasks.

4

The Formation
Stage

First the blade, and then the ear . . .

More has been learned about small-group development in the last two decades than in the previous two millennia. The human potential movement, with its encounter groups, sensitivity groups, growth labs, and organizational development studies, has fueled an intense amount of research into group development. What happens from the first day a small group gathers until it finally reaches its goal(s)? Given a wide variety of group types and accompanying goals, social scientists have been able to chart discernible and predictable patterns of development. The pastor does not have to start from scratch or proceed by trial and error. Premature failures can be minimized by "going to school" on the experience of reliable scientific sources.

Group Theory

Although the social scientists may describe the developmental steps or phases of groups in different ways, some common threads are quite visible. To give some examples:

Tuckman—Groups move from testing to conflict to cohesion to functioning (Lawrence B. Rosenfeld, *Human Interaction in the Small Group Setting*, p. 52; Charles E. Merrill Publishing Co., 1973)

Wilson—Groups move from dependence to conflict to cohesion to work (Stephen Wilson, *Informal Groups,* Prentice-Hall, 1978)

Mills—Groups move from encounter to testing to negotiating to production (Theodore M. Mills, *The Sociology of Small Groups,* Prentice-Hall, 1967)

Cohen and Smith—Groups move from acquaintance to anxiety to definition to transference to defensiveness to conflict to norm crystallization to shared leadership to less defensiveness to experimentation to potency (A. M. Cohen and R. D. Smith, *The Critical Incident in Growth Groups: Theory and Practice,* University Associates, 1976)

Clinebell—Groups move from anxiety to testing to connecting attempts to euphoria to frustration to questioning to risking to trusting to effective growth/work to closing (Howard Clinebell, *The People Dynamic,* Harper & Row, 1972)

Hinton and Reitz—Groups move from forming (Dependence) to storming (Conflict) to norming (Cohesion) to performing (Role Function) (B. L. Hinton and H. J. Reitz (comps.), *Groups and Organizations,* Wadsworth Publishing Co., 1971)

Egan—Groups move from milling around to hostility to inability to work (Gerard Egan, *Face to Face,* Brooks/Cole Publishing Co., 1973)

Bennis and Shepherd—Groups move

From dependence	To interdependence
1. submission (flight)	1. enchantment (flight)
2. counterdependence (flight)	2. disenchantment (flight)
3. resolution (catharsis)	3. consensual validation

(Bennis and Shepherd, "A Theory of Group Development," *Human Relations,* National Training Laboratories, 1956, pp. 415–437)

These authors' independent studies reveal an amazing consensus about the developmental stages in group formation. Their conclusions also deal with other common critical issues with which the groups they studied had to deal, such as dependency, power, authority, intimacy, love, and individuality. As I reflect on the wide variety of intentional Christian communities or church groups in which I have participated, I recognize that these same factors were at work. A group progresses through these stages, whether in a prayer group or a task/action group. Each group moves at its own pace. It may move with speed and ease through certain aspects of a stage or struggle with great difficulty through another phase, but, nevertheless, the stages will be there.

My own observation of the formation stage of small-group development shows the following progression: discovery, romance, struggle, and investment.

At the time the group first gathers, an implicit covenant is in place. This is shaped by the advertising, interpretation, and invitation of the group conveners. It may be specific and in writing, but more often it is not. Even if the contract is in writing, each person will give a distinct interpretation to it. The covenant stands as implicit. Only after the group has gone through the throes of interacting and testing can members really emotionally own an explicit contract. Only after they have jelled with their own identity as a group can they invest toward the fulfillment of their desired goal.

Jesus' experience with his disciples shows the progression and their own struggle to become a group. The implicit covenant grew out of their curiosity and trust of Jesus as well as his invitation. A period of *discovery* ensued as they came to know him and one another. *Romance* was fed by healings, miracles, and their popularity with large crowds. The *struggle* was precipitated by Jesus' teaching and actions regarding the cost and nature of discipleship. This came to a head following the feeding of the multitudes when he spoke of himself as the bread (John 6). He taught that one must deny self, take up a cross, and follow. Many followers left him because "the sayings were too hard" for them. They had other expectations of him. Jesus turned to the Twelve and asked, "Will you also go away?" Peter's response: "Where else will we go? You alone have the words of eternal life," cements the *explicit covenant.* They then *invested* themselves in mutual ministry and *functioned* together until the Passover meal.

As we make closer examination of the developmental stages, we will also discover some critical dynamics at work. The group will move through the dynamic levels of anxiety, trust, and power as it begins its journey.

1. *Discovery*

The road begins with *anxiety.* "No matter what you do in a group for its first six hours together," says a friend, "the group will be preoccupied with sniffing!" People will be asking themselves: "Is this a safe place for me to be?" "Will I be accepted?" "Will I feel some sense of worth or value?" "Will I be manipulated or overpowered?" "Will the others extend their goodwill toward me?" "Will I be expected to do something that will reveal my inadequacies?"

The process of *trust* building involves self-disclosure and affirmation. Stories are told and stories are heard. Trust is built as persons who gather for the first time let others know little by little who they are. They begin with the most familiar items: vocation, residence, family. As they feel safer, they unravel a little more history: childhood, aspirations, values. Then they may share some hidden feelings: fear, tearful pain, anxiety, joys, and hopes for the future. With each step, acceptance and affirmation build trust so that the persons really feel that the group is *with* them and *for* them.

The gospel is the story of God's self-disclosure to his people. Jesus reveals what God is like—that he is trustworthy. This theological foundation says that the order of the universe is built on trustworthiness. The God who discloses himself as one worthy of our trust presents a signal for our own human order and invites us to enter into relationships with the body of Christ through self-disclosure. We can entrust our selves to the group. Love, trust, affirmation, confession, forgiveness, healing, and care become more than theological jargon. Jesus' activity was open and vulnerable. We can dare to present our stories to a faith community whose response becomes a means of God's grace to us.

The critical factor of *power* centers on the exercise of leadership within the group. Newly formed groups tend to be very dependent on the leader, which isn't necessarily bad. This does not mean that the leader is one who gives answers, but it does mean that the leader skillfully guides the group in its developmental process. Dependency calls for more directive leadership. A leader who will not exercise initiative can paralyze the group and block its growth. "What do you want to do and/or be" falls far short of "Let me suggest some ways we could work to discover what we want to do and/or be!"

2. Romance

The discovery road leads on to *romance*. The members feel euphoric, comfortable with one another, and excited about their new friendships. But this is just the lull before the storm. A struggle is about to begin.

Myra Thompson-Flood described her experience in the Potter's House mission group of the Church of the Saviour of Washington, D.C.: "At first we were filled with excitement. It was a time of exploration; of how to do the job. We were having warm and loving feelings. A 'glow' prevailed. By the end of the first year the honeymoon was over. Interpersonal relationships needed to be worked through to some resolution and common division of labor."

3. Struggle

The euphoria of romance sooner or later falls off into struggle. The good feelings based on common affinity cannot last. The struggle arises when people discover that other Christians also

have wants, or flaws, or personality quirks. The context of
honesty has freed them to assert their own individuality.

> When the group first meets, the situation is new; members are
> anxious and uncertain about what to expect. A good deal of time
> is spent "feeling each other out." When the newness of the
> situation begins to wear off, group members start to assert their
> individuality. . . . The group re-forms in order to pursue its
> functions. (Lawrence B. Rosenfeld, *Human Interaction in the
> Small Group Setting,* p. 52; Charles E. Merrill Publishing Co.,
> 1973)

As the formation stage develops from romance through struggle it moves back through the critical issues of power, trust, and
anxiety. The power issue turns to counterdependency, to questioning or attacking the leader. Those of us who have worked
on the five-day training conference circuit are all very well
aware of day *three!* (Most painfully aware!) Day one is a day
of orientation and getting acquainted. Day two involves agenda
building. Day three is the time to attack the agenda and leadership and take over the conference! After some negotiation and
reconciliation, day four produces some good work; by day five,
the participants' energies are spent on disengagement.

Participants will be less trusting during the struggle phase and
may take some distance from one another. Anxiety will increase
as they fear that the group may abort and not push through to
resolution and ownership of the covenant, toward the real purpose of the group.

4. *Investment*

If the members of the group will stay with one another and
with the struggle to become a group, they will move to a deep
love and clear covenant. Community will burst upon them as
gift, and not something they have earned or forged for themselves. Here our theology of the church serves us well. God's gift
of grace reconciles us, brings us together, and unites us in the
bond of Jesus Christ.

As the group moves with covenant in hand toward the final leg of the formation stage—toward effective functioning—it will find that anxiety turns to hope. Members' visions are confirmed and together. The supportive values that underlie the visions are congruent. Their individuality has been established, personally and corporately, which leads them into a great deal of freedom. And, finally, the power issue has resolved itself in shared leadership. This does not mean that the group is leaderless or that leadership is shared equally. It does mean that leader functions have been defined and accepted. There still may be a single leader and enabler, or leadership may be shared by a core team of two or three persons, or it may be passed around. At least the life of the group no longer depends on the leader. The group will have picked up its own oars.

The covenant community has a rich theological heritage. Whereas contract may seem to center on human relationships, covenant popularly focuses on the sacred relationships with God and with brothers and sisters in the faith.

The Old Testament concept of covenant was the ratification of an agreement through an external act. One ancient covenant reveals two parties to the covenant drinking each other's blood, symbolizing their brotherhood. The custom of "cutting a covenant" severed an animal in half, separating the two parts, with the agreeing parties passing between. They seemed to say, "So be it with you if you break the agreement!" The sacrificial meal was another way to ratify a covenant. Eating together secured the bond.

One ancient covenant service which some groups use is the covenant of salt. It can be shared while at a meal, where eating is the symbol of friendship. The preservation function of salt symbolizes the lasting nature of the covenant.

The New Testament covenant signifies Christ's poured-out, self-giving love. Sharing the Sacrament of Holy Communion in the group setting, when administered by you as pastor, raises both the witness and judgment—how are we pouring self-giving love here? We make a covenant to be with and for each other, where love does not have to be earned. The covenant stands in contrast to many human relations models of groups, which worship at the altar of individual self-understanding or personal growth, at all costs.

The Pastor's Enabling Skills

As pastor, you may find your ministry at the formation stage of group life expressed in several ways. You may be the on-site convener and leader of a newly gathered group which you will either continue to lead or pass the leadership along to an emerging lay leader in the group. Sometimes that person may actually be in an apprentice role.

The other facet of ministry is the training and support of lay leaders whose intentions may be on locating in a group from the beginning.

Leader skills that operate in trust building are so crucial because this stage lends itself to manipulation. Many pastors and lay leaders push a group into premature self-disclosure. "The more honest and deep the sharing goes," they say, "the better." But few people are really helped by having their masks pried off or their onion peeled down. One rule of thumb I have followed in leading groups is always to let the participant's own perceived trust level of the group dictate the depth of the sharing. Private matters should only be shared when one feels that the group is a safe place in which to share them.

The need to be included will push many people to play games just to get in, even if they go too deep. The wise leader who can legitimize semi-participation or nonparticipation by openly recognizing it, then allowing opportunities to say "Pass" or "Stop," will avoid violating another's personhood. Going around the circle or saying, "Now let's all . . . ," sets traps for people. They need to be freed to take responsibility for themselves, including what they will or will not share in a group. The request, for instance, for participants to relate "*a* significant experience of . . ." is much more enabling than "Share *the most* significant experience of . . ." The participant then has options from which to select.

The skilled leader can deal with the anxiety by quickly establishing some protective structure, or ground rules: "We won't ask 'why' questions." "Pass, if what we ask of you makes you feel uncomfortable." Or the leader may normalize the anxiety: "Everyone feels uncertain. That's normal and human." Some simple exercises can be designed that will assist the participants to name the anxiety. One such exercise suggests that you imagine that you are riding home with a trusted friend after the group series has concluded. The group has been a bad experience and you are telling your friend about it. The exercise will bring one's fears to the surface, where they can be recognized and dealt with.

The pastor can offer helpful devices and structured experiences to move a group to a level beyond the mere coffee-hour chitchat. Ample material with specific "how to" suggestions is available. Good training programs not only attempt to provide the leader with methods, structured experiences, and rules of thumb but also with some discerning helps on how, when, and under what circumstances to use them. Surgical tools may be used in two ways: to help heal persons or to cut them to pieces. Likewise, sensitivity and encounter tools can be dangerous unless the leader has self-awareness and an awareness of what is really happening or needs to happen in the group. The pastor can offer guidance for lay leaders on when and how to use certain structural tools from the bag!

Of utmost importance are listening and feeding information back in such a way that the discloser really feels heard and affirmed. Simple exercises that repeat what others say (to their satisfaction) without judging or interpreting can foster growth in the group as a whole.

The most important pastoral support phase for the lay leader is when the group moves off the heights of romance into struggle. Here the critical dynamic of power shift hits the vulnerable gut of the unaware lay leader. Power shifts from dependency on the leader to distancing, competing, or open hostility. If the leader knows that the issue is not his or her worth as a person or ability as a leader, he or she will not run away but will stay in there with the group. This often is a lonely or bewildering time, one that calls for sensitive pastoral care.

Some leaders will precipitate a crisis to help the group move off the dead center of dependency on the leader and romance. A friend of mine was preparing to attend a vocal music clinic. He was forewarned: "Watch the guest conductor. The first two days he will praise and compliment you. On the third day he will throw down his baton in disgust and walk out. Then after a brief time he will come back, and things really happen from that time on!"

Another example of this method can be seen in an account of the development of an adult confirmation class that was conducted by the staff of St. Mark's Episcopal Church in Washington.

> The growth in self-understanding at the conference was as usual, achieved at the cost of *intensifying the strain in the relationship between the members of the class and the staff.* In the weeks just prior to the conference, the participants had indicated increasing disappointment with the progress the class was making and had focused this disappointment on the staff.
>
> The negative feeling of the class towards the staff was heightened by the role play used to dramatize the problem under consideration for the weekend. Each small group was to have its own role play without an audience. "In this role play," the members of the class were told, "you will play a person very much like yourself, a person with your name and personality. Only the role player from the staff will assume a different name and different characteristics." Then each small group was instructed to think of itself as a group of friends who *have gathered to honor a particularly valued* friend named Tom Fletcher, or Ann Church, these characters to be portrayed by members of the staff. Tom and Ann were described to the group as people who had found job satisfaction, sound family relationships and close friends, and as responsible citizens with a social conscience.

These were people who had fulfilled all, or most, of the aspirations evidenced by members of the class in their previous sessions. The assignment for each small group was to plan a party and gift presentation for Tom and Ann to demonstrate the affection and appreciation of the group for this person's contributions to their lives.

A crisis was precipitated in the role plays when each *Tom and Ann refused the gift,* confessing that until this point life had been a sham. In fact, the way of life that had been pursued by these characters had been merely a way of *covering up* their discovery that life is meaningless. From now on, the Toms and Anns insisted, they would value only absolute honesty, refusing to participate in most of their former activities and relationships because they have no meaning. (James R. Adams and Celia Allison Hahn, *A Way to Belong,* p. 9; Alban Institute, Mt. St. Alban, Washington, D.C., 1980; emphasis added)

This example is rather strong, and I would not necessarily endorse its use in every group situation or by all leaders. It does serve to illustrate, however, the counterdependence phenomenon. Most group leaders will simply want to be aware of it, work with it, and not allow themselves to be crushed by it.

As the group moves out of its struggle and into a healthy investment, I can't overstate the importance of working through a renegotiated covenant through which the group can invest. The more explicit it is, the more helpful it will be. Write it out. Test it. Select a name for it or for the group. Create a symbol for it. Celebrate it. Put together a liturgy that lifts it onto "sacred ground."

Let us now probe the depths of covenant making.

Practice in Churches—Covenant Making

The greatest service that pastoral leadership can provide its groups is to assist them in drafting clear covenants. I cannot overemphasize the importance of these efforts. No substitute exists for a good, agreed-upon covenant. A clear covenant will help a group establish its *identity*. As persons, our behavior flows out of desires to confirm our own self-image. If our self-image is blurred or diffused, our behavior will be erratic. The same can be said for a small group. Knowing "who we are" will set the course for "what we will do."

A clear covenant establishes *intentional* goals and directions. Just as healthy persons live and act out of their will and intentions, so groups are able to decide about their behavior and tasks, moving with maximum power.

Covenants also provide *freedom*. People frequently get caught up in a myriad of activities, trying to be and do everything others expect of them. Being unable to say no, they soon find their energies dissipated to the point where they are effective in nothing. Groups can get caught in the same rut.

One of my most frustrating experiences in a house church was with a group that had not come to a contract consensus. We operated out of varying expectations the participants held. As a result, every meeting turned into an evaluation session on "what's wrong with the group" and a planning meeting deciding "what we should do next time." Once we took the time to establish a covenant for a two-month period, we were freed from evaluating and deciding. We functioned effectively for those two months.

Groups with covenants can focus their energy, having some basis for saying, "This is what we can do, and this is what we can't do." Participants sometimes expect too much from a group. They must realize that no group can fulfill all one's needs and aspirations. Knowing the limits as well as the possibilities is a very freeing thing!

Evaluating and *celebration* become possible for groups that function with clear covenants. We tend to resent evaluation that comes from the outside or from the top. When a contract that has been drawn by the group becomes the standard for evaluation, the interest and the motivation of the group are heightened! If the group has been functioning within the life of a congregation, the contracting and evaluating are placed in a larger context. The integration of the group into the larger congregation is assured.

Besides, now the group has some real basis for celebrating.

"We blew it, Lord. Have mercy upon us."

"Thank you, Lord, for helping us."

"Come, let's rejoice together, Alleluia!"

"We are still concerned about . . . and pray for . . ."

"We affirm and believe from our experience that God . . ."

If we really believe that worship is a response to God's activity in our lives, experience can be taken seriously. And experiences that grow out of a group's expressed covenant to be and do are concrete enough to make celebration come alive!

1. *Types of Covenants*

A contract is a contract, you say? Not quite. The data collected by Project Base Church over a three-year period reveal four distinct types of covenants.

An *assumed* covenant has never been considered by the group as a whole and has never been explicitly stated. When each person in the group assumes that he or she knows what the covenant is, the group risks painful conflict, because unmet expectations will almost certainly cause frustration and anger.

Some groups, however, can function adequately for a time with only an implicit contract. A clear vision presented by the group's convener creates an implicit contract. The overwhelming needs of the participants can also set the contract. Our data show, for instance, that 65 percent of the people who come into house churches do so out of a deep hunger for community, sharing, and intimacy within a primary small group. An obvious need or task around which people rally can also form an implicit contract. Assisting victims of natural disasters, diseases, and social conflicts focuses and mobilizes the energy of a group.

But time will catch up with most groups. An assumed contract will spend itself, leaving the group either to disband or to negotiate a more explicit one.

The *purchased* covenant is another common type. In the purchased contract, most of the details are set up and offered. The potential participant considers the offer and its terms, then buys in by signing up for the group.

A church decides to concentrate its fall program into a spectrum of group offerings. The officers determine that some will center on personal growth, some on Bible or theme studies, and some on mission action. The offerings are publicized to start on X date, run for X weeks, meet at X place for X hours with X leading, using X resource and following X group process. Folks can decline the offering or sign up for their preference. They purchase a set, closed contract. The advantages of this contract lie in the minimum amount of time spent in the early meetings with the struggles for group formation. That energy has already gone into the selection process.

A specific program resource (tape, film, book, or guide) can also occasion a group covenant. My experience of producing, testing, and distributing *The Church in Small Groups,* an audio-cassette resource, shows that a structured program with a built-in contract can be very enabling. To avoid trouble, the contract must also be tested for ownership early in the program. The test groups that aborted revealed a common trait: their implicit contract, under which they *really* operated, had been set by their previous experience as a group or by publicity that did not match the contract offered at the beginning of the taped program. Thus they never really "purchased" or "bought into" the contract.

A strong and skilled leader could also occasion a purchased covenant, which is tied to the group members' dependency. A group may say: "We're not sure what we want or what is good for us. But we trust you and believe that your insight and experience will help you make the proper decisions about what we do and how we do it. We buy into your leading us as seems best to you. We will tell you if you go too far, not far enough, or in the wrong direction. In the meantime, go to it!"

The *imposed* covenant is harder to take. Once the person is in a larger "system," the powers that be determine what group the person will be in and what it must do. If the system is a voluntary one, the individual will weigh the value of continued membership in the system. If the person values it highly enough, he or she may choose to go along, but the group will go through the developing cycle until the members own it.

The geographically constructed parish zone plan of many congregations defines the groups and imposes the contract. The well-documented fact that few of these plans have worked over the years reveals their fatal flaw. Power exercised at the top with no optional decisions at the bottom spells zero motivation.

The most common type of covenant is the *negotiated* one. After the group has been together long enough to have established a high trust level and to struggle through their reservations, the members can be open about their hopes for and expectations of the group. It is extremely important for each person to be frank about one's personal "agenda" so that open negotiating can take place. Both the possibilities and the limitations of the group can be owned. The more explicitly the contract is stated, the better. If some time limit has been established, evaluation can then lead to a new stage of contracting at a later date.

One word of caution is in order. We have discovered that a too-ambitious and exacting contract written too early in the group's life can frustrate it and produce all kinds of feelings of inadequacy. Telling our stories, hearing each other out, and supporting each other may be enough contract until the group is ready to move. Trust building is even essential at the beginning of a task/action group if it is going to accomplish its contracted goal(s).

2. *Process of Negotiation*

Groups and their leaders know that they ought to have a covenant! But how to negotiate a covenant from scratch can be

a difficult and elusive endeavor. The following step-by-step procedure can bring a fruitful covenant.

a. *Surfacing.* Any person who comes into a new group situation brings something. One cannot come in blank. So the first
step in contracting is to bring to the surface people's needs,
fears, hopes, visions, expectations, values, and faith affirmations
—placing them out in the open for the group to see and com-
pare.

As you or I come to a new group situation, for instance, we
bring the need to be heard, accepted, loved, and affirmed as a
person. We want to feel valued. We want to belong and to know
that this is a safe place for us to be. We may fear that others will
reject us when they get to know us, or that we will be used or
manipulated, or that confidences will be violated. We bring
dreams, hopes, and visions on how our life can count in ministry
to other people who have needs—perhaps through this group.
So we expect the group to spend energy beyond its own maintenance. We bring our values of loyalty and trust, and even a need
for private space as well as intimate community. We bring faith
affirmations: God acts and lives in and through his people, so
we would like the group to include some expressions of praise,
thanksgiving, and intercession.

The group that ignores these basic human factors in its hurry
to get on with the contract is taking an unnecessary risk. People
function at a deep energy level to get their needs met and express
their values. If the group contract is not a fulfilling avenue,
members will block and sabotage the endeavor. If their inner
"stuff" does not come out straight in the beginning, it will come
out sideways later and unconsciously impair the group's functioning. Surfacing is an attempt to let it come out straight.

Examples:

Suggest that people simply complete the statements, "I want
. . . I need . . . I offer . . ."

Invite participants to write or describe their spiritual journey,
identifying where they are now. They might divide it into periods of life, giving fuller detail on the period of life they are in now.

Give everyone a sheet of newsprint with the verbal instruction: "Fold it in half, then tear a hole in the middle large enough for your head. Write on the front 'What I want or hope the group will be' and, on the back, 'How I can make that happen.' Then wear the signs and interview each other in mixer fashion."

Dialogue in one-to-one fashion.

Draw a picture in three parts: "Where I have been, where I would like to go, what keeps me from getting there." Share the pictures with the group.

Create a symbol for what you would like this group to be. Then explain it to the group.

Take a fantasy trip with the whole group to another place and time (new city or old European village) and imagine how and what the group is doing.

b. *Clustering.* Once the participants' concerns have surfaced, the next step clusters or groups the concerns together. Visualization is extremely important at this step, to avoid losing the concerns of the less verbal participants.

Record on newsprint what each person reported, then cluster the responses by drawing connecting arrows or distinguishing signs. If symbols have been drawn or created, they can be moved and grouped.

As everyone works at the process, from two to five dominant threads will emerge to form a skeleton on which to hang specific covenant flesh.

c. *Concretizing.* Now you can be specific—and the more specific the better. Nail down times, places, behavior, objectives, and so on. Test whether the covenant identifies the group, says what it will do, holds individuals accountable, and gives a clear basis for later evaluation.

d. *Testing.* Once the covenant is completed, ask the group: "Now how do you feel about it? Can you commit your energy to it?"

You may ask for verbal responses or utilize a nonverbal approach. Place the covenant on the floor in the center of the room. Ask people to stand in a position (close or far away) that reflects how they feel about it. Let any who want to talk about where they are standing do so.

Or have each person record a number (one to ten), from "one —very dissatisfied" to "ten—very satisfied" and discuss the numbers. Either test will reveal anyone who is at odds with the rest of the group, as well as where the group as a whole feels it stands. Many times a few persons get left out, or the covenant may diverge from the path the group really wants to follow. Thus, testing is an important step to keep the group on target.

e. *Symbolizing.* If the group cannot agree on a single symbol that focuses its identity and purpose, the covenant is probably too diverse and inclusive. On the other hand, if a group has difficulty constructing a covenant, members might *begin* by attempting to select a symbol. I have seen some groups start with symbol selection and find it a very enabling exercise.

A symbol provides clarity and focus. It can also provide an additional check for group ownership or provide the basis for minor revision. Once the symbol is selected, it can be constructed or formed by having the participants place themselves in a physical position that describes the symbol.

One group explored possible symbols with these suggestions: a cup, a series of candles, a wheel with spokes, motion. They finally formed the symbol by clasping a common cup with their joined right hands while their left hands rested on the left shoulder of the person next to them (in wheel-like fashion). Then they marched clockwise while singing a praise song.

Such a symbol can be repeatedly put together at each gathering or in response to a significant event or moment.

If groups construct a tangible symbol, it can be carried from meeting to meeting, helping to set the environment. This is significant because one issue growing out of the house church movement has been, "Do people need a place?" Do religious communities need a building in order to function and grow? Do groups need to stake out "holy ground" or "holy space"? Many say yes. My own conclusion is that people need to symbolize their experience, existence, and place. A church building is most visible in a property- and real estate-oriented society. If, however, religious communities learn to create symbols growing out of their own experience, their compulsive desire to build buildings will be minimized. Portable or instant symbols carry powerful meanings that can enrich the covenanting process as well as provide a centering and security for the person on a religious journey.

f. *Celebrating.* Small groups within the Christian tradition have a powerful history and custom of celebration. Celebration naturally follows symbolizing. Participants are given the opportunity to commit themselves to the contract, in the presence of God and each other.

Worship can provide the spiritual glue that holds a group together. What better way to launch the group experience than to prepare and conduct a worship/liturgy that centers on the symbol of the covenant! A common element of the liturgy (song, dance, chant, pledge) could be reaffirmed at each subsequent meeting.

3. *Ingredients of a Covenant*

No two covenants look alike; one cannot prescribe what must always be included in a covenant. Many covenants do contain a number of common ingredients. This rather exhaustive listing offers suggestions and ideas to covenanting groups. All do not have to be incorporated into each group.

a. *Duration.* A covenant that is set for X weeks or months provides a built-in mechanism for evaluating. The evaluation may feed into the recovenanting process. Or a time limit can assist a group to terminate. In a fast-moving society, people are more likely to become involved in the first place if they know the time limits. A limited time covenant also provides a breathing spell in which people can get out gracefully or come in without disrupting the group.

Most groups that practice covenanting set the duration from three to twelve months. Groups with three-month covenant intervals function acceptably, providing they renegotiate for a new stage. If they construct new groups, they will need a covenanting period longer than three months.

b. *Meetings.* State specific time, place, schedule, and meal or snack procedure.

c. *Attendance.* While all the covenants encourage regular attendance, some include specific procedures: "I will always call if I am unable to attend."

d. *Leadership.* Will one person serve as designated leader? Will two or three share the responsibility? Will all take turns? (When hosting?) Or will the leadership functions be shared by all as it becomes the enabling thing to do?

e. *Faith Affirmations.* Since many people are motivated to participate out of some deeply rooted faith beliefs and commitments, their affirmations are incorporated into the covenant. Most frequently the affirmations appear as a credo preamble: "Since we believe . . . we agree to . . ."

f. *Participants.* One experimental group covenanted to be "intergenerational." Yet that needed to be spelled out further. "We will alternate every other week between adult and intergenerational meetings."

Some churches openly attempt to create as much diversity as possible in groups, and the covenant reflects it.

Whether a group is open or closed to visitors or new members can become a significant issue. Some groups are always open (especially the worship-oriented ones); some are always closed (high-intensity, personal growth groups); some are closed for the duration of the contract, then open for the new stage. One group for which new participants were an issue compromised. "We will only bring new visitors when we have first checked with and have permission of the group to do so."

g. *Exits.* The dropout leaves much unfinished business, for both the person and the group. One covenant statement addressed the problem by stating, "I will participate through the duration of the group and will not drop out unless I first notify the group in person of my intention to do so."

h. *Worship.* The basic marks of the church find their way into covenants. The intention to engage in worship may spell out patterns of praise and prayer or the conditions and frequency of the use of the Sacraments. One group included its desire to pray regularly in the contract. "When visitors come," they said, "we don't want to hassle over, apologize for, or justify our prayer efforts. The covenant states what we do. If visitors can 'stomach' us, they can share with us. But we won't reduce our worship practices to the lowest common denominator of acceptability."

i. *Study.* Both the source for study (Bible, book, theme, etc.) and the process for study (teaching, dialogue, research, etc.) can find their way into a covenant.

j. *Ministry.* "For the next two months our mission outreach will focus on relating to international people within the city." This general statement set the direction for the group's ministry. Specific strategies could also have been incorporated.

k. *Fellowship.* Building a community of trust calls for some well-understood behavioral guidelines.

"I will try to hear you."

"When you get in touch with deep feelings, I will not run away from you, or try to talk you out of them, or fix the situation for you, but will be with you."

"I will not probe or ask 'why' questions."

"I will keep confidences shared here."

"I will not discuss what went on in our meeting outside the gathering—even with another group member."

"I will love and affirm you as a person, calling forth your unique gifts."

"I will say 'Stop' when I do not want to share further."

l. *Personal Disciplines.* Promises can be made to the whole group to pray daily for each other, to meditate or read the Bible daily, to tithe, attend church, and so forth.

m. *Money and Things.* Economic sharing in groups is one of the new frontiers for the church, especially in a postaffluent society where stewardship of the earth's resources is vitally important.

n. *Connections.* The group may spell out its relationship to the larger congregation or some other church structure.

Example: a church group related to the Aibonito, Puerto Rico, Mennonite Church incorporated this connectional statement in their covenant:

> We ask the Mennonite congregation in Aibonito to consider the base group as an integral and legitimate part of its ministry.
> A. We ask the church council to approve the purposes of the base group.
> B. On a Sunday we request the congregation to commission the base group for a period of six months for the indicated purposes. The same day we request fifteen minutes of the adult classes to discuss with them our purposes.
> C. We request the Aibonito congregation to counsel us about our life as a group. Bob Martin will be the normal contact person between the congregation and the base group.
> D. We ask the congregation to evaluate with us the experiences of the group at the end of six months. We will make decisions about the future of the group according to the results of the evaluation.
> E. The members of the group will be with the congregation in worship on Sunday mornings, except for ordinary legitimate reasons. Participation in other activities of the congregation will depend on the individual group members.
> F. To symbolize our unity with the congregation we request that at least one family of the church be with us when we celebrate a baptism, foot washing, or the Lord's Supper.

o. *Decisions.* How shall the group make decisions about its life? By voting? By consensus? By delegating decision making to a small number of trusted "elders"?

p. *Personal Covenants.* The Agora Community in Minneapolis and Ecumenikos in Kansas City invite individuals to write their own personal covenant statements, which are in turn heard and ratified by the community. Sometimes this is done as a response to a corporate covenant. It may be specific: "We offer to keep the children of each family in this group for one weekend during the next three months." Or it may be general: "I covenant with this community my time and energy for mutual effort and support toward a faith community in which God's love is expressed by love of one's fellow man" (from a covenant in Ecumenikos).

q. *Evaluation.* The time and method for evaluating may be specified. "Will we evaluate ourselves? Or invite someone from the outside to assist us? Or share with other groups in an overall evaluation process?"

4. *Sample Covenants*

From the Mennonite group in Aibonito, Puerto Rico:

> We confess that Jesus Christ is Lord.
>
> Because God in Christ has made us His people, we covenant to have fellowship with each other and with God, to serve each other and the world, and to proclaim the Gospel of God's kingdom.
>
> A. Fellowship: We will meet together once a week. Together we will learn, sing, eat, discipline, exhort, pray, share, decide, share the Lord's Supper, and give.
>
> B. Service: In the group we will discern and develop our gifts to serve God's people and the world, both as individuals and as a group.
>
> C. Testimony: We will share with persons in the world what God has done in Christ, in individuals, and in the base group. We will invite them to follow Christ Jesus the Lord with us.

From Covenant Groups in the National Presbyterian Church in Washington, D.C.:

> Covenant Groups are an expression of our life in Christ, and cannot reach their potential unless He is an active member of the

group. Our life and strength flow from Him; therefore we can take joy in His presence and express what He is accomplishing in our group as a member of it.

His Word is our Guide to all of life and therefore It should be used as the group feels the need. It is out of His Word that we identify the following covenant dynamics:

1. The covenant of Affirmation (unconditional love, agape love)

   "There is nothing you have done, or will do, that will make me stop loving you. I may not agree with your actions, but I will love you as a person and do all I can to hold you up in God's affirming love."

2. The covenant of Availability

   "Anything I have—time, energy, insight, possessions—are at your disposal if you need them. I give these to you in a priority of covenant over other noncovenant demands. As part of this availability I pledge regularity of time, whether in prayer, or in an agreed-upon meeting time."

3. The covenant of Prayer

   "I covenant to pray for you in some regular fashion, believing that our caring Father wishes His children to pray for one another and ask Him for the blessings they need."

4. The covenant of Openness

   "I promise to strive to become a more open person, disclosing my feelings, my struggles, my joys, and my hurts to you as well as I am able. The degree to which I do so implies that I cannot make it without you, that I trust you with my needs, and that I need you. This is to affirm your worth to me as a person. In other words, I need you!"

5. The covenant of Sensitivity

   "Even as I desire to be known and understood by you, I covenant to be sensitive to you and to your needs to the best of my ability. I will try to 'hear you, see you and feel where you are,' to draw you out of the pit of discouragement or withdrawal."

6. The covenant of Honesty

   "I will try to 'mirror back' to you what I am hearing you say and feel. If this means risking pain for either of us, I will trust our relationship enough to take that risk, realizing it is in 'speaking the truth in love, that we grow up in every way into Christ who is the Head.' I will try to express this honesty, to 'meter it,' according to what I perceive the circumstances to be."

7. The covenant of Confidentiality

"I will promise to keep whatever is shared within the confines of the group, in order to provide the 'permissive atmosphere' necessary for openness."

From The Early Church (a house church) in New Jersey:

As Christ followers relying on the Holy Spirit we covenant with one another to become an inclusive, intergenerational community of faith, seeking to understand and to do God's will through:

1. daily communication with God in prayer
2. regular study of the Bible and other materials
3. weekly worship experiences with the covenanted group
4. calling forth of each other's gifts
5. an emphasis on small-group structures
6. a development of interpersonal relationships through both affirming and admonishing
7. sharing of our spiritual gifts and material possessions
8. support and service to church, community, and world.

We pledge to strive toward a life-style that does not conform to the standards of this world, but allows God to transform us, acknowledging always our continuing need for God's forgiveness and forgiveness by the community of faith.

From the West Hills Presbyterian Church of Omaha, Nebraska:

GROUP COVENANT

Our group goals are: _____

_____

_____

What we intend to study is _____

We have covenanted together to meet for ____ weeks, at which time we will review and evaluate our group.

We will meet each week on _____. We   will
                          (day of week)
begin at _____ and close at _____ .
        (time)   (time)

A typical schedule will look like: _____
                                   _____
                                   _____

Ground Rules
Food: _____   Dress: _____
Children: _____   Place: _____
Absence: _____   Leadership
                              Responsibility: _____

Individual Preparation and
Responsibility: _____ Visitors: _____

Evaluation   Reevaluation
Procedures: _____   Time: _____

Telephone   Open (new people can come
Interruptions: _____   any time) or Closed Group
                              (after third meeting, no
                              new members): _____

Decision Making: _____   Ministry (group or support in-
                              dividual): _____

Personal Disciplines: _____

I will try, with God's help, to be a regular, faithful, involved,
caring member of this Covenant Group.

                    Signed _____

5

The Functioning Stage

Then the full corn shall appear . . .

Harvesttime! What a thrill! All the planter's energy and vision now come to fruition. The price that has been paid by the pastor in the investment in small groups is now paying off. The pastor who says, "It is a lot of work, but it is worth it," has come through the joy of harvest. The increased yield comes in authentic relationships, healthy people, committed disciples, biblically and theologically aware laypersons, and intangible expressions of ministry and outreach.

Group Theory

Once the group has developed its life through an agreed-upon covenant (written or informal), its members can freely invest themselves toward its purposes. This new functioning stage for the church-oriented group can be examined in two ways: through the lenses of its actual behavior and through the lenses of the four basic marks of the church.

The first perspective from which to view the function stage of the group is a *behavioral* one. What is really happening here?

Communication takes place, both verbal and nonverbal.

Stories are told.

Needs are being met (or people become frustrated when they are not met).

Decisions are being made.

Feelings surface.

Conflicts arise and are resolved or ignored.

Entrances and exits of people require new trust building and grieving energy.

Gifts are expressed.

Feelings surface.

Breakthrough happens.

Evaluation and contracting lead to new arenas of group expression.

Group maintenance calls for the continuing awareness of what is happening in the group in terms of process. Many of those initial needs, personalities, and visions will continue to play themselves out in the nitty-gritty of the functioning group. One leader observed, "No matter what else is going on in any given group, each participant will be working to get his or her needs met." The needs are not bad. They are part of God's good creation.

So many events have a powerful effect on the group. The entering or exiting member may stop a group in midstream. The new member does not know the group's history and can reduce the trust level. Time needs to be taken to implant the new member in the group. (Some groups are intentionally closed for designated periods of time because of this effect). The exiting member may leave the group with unresolved conflict, a leadership vacuum, guilt over not having supported him or her, or grief over a significant loss.

The *basic marks of the church* form the second perspective from which to view the functioning stage of a group: fellowship, nurture, worship, and mission.

A look at recent attempts to develop house churches may be instructive for congregations that work with small groups. What makes the house church different from the traditional prayer group, sharing group, or task group is its self-conscious identity as "church." It attempts to function with the four marks of the church: worship, Christian nurture, fellowship, and ministry. The house church movement has sent a message to the larger church. The message says: "We are church. We are willing to bear the full marks of the church in the single, primary cell. Our worship is not second class because it does not take place in a sanctuary. Our nurture is vital even though we do not follow prescribed curriculum. Our mission efforts have power even though we do not apply large numbers of people or much money."

Look at the way basic communities view themselves. They are not just prayer groups and not just action groups. They see themselves as bearing in microcosm the full marks of the church while at the same time maintaining a connection to some larger expression of the church, whether to congregations or to a cluster of the base groups.

Although many house churches attempt to divide their energy equally around the four marks of wholeness, only a few that function within congregations actually achieve such balance. Groups in churches may convene around one of the particular marks where they concentrate their energies. One of the exciting learnings from the house church movement for the congregation is that even though a group may focus upon a particular mark (study, fellowship, or worship), the other marks can interplay in a supportive way.

Let us examine more closely the four functional marks of the basic, intentional Christian community.

1. *Fellowship*

The supportive fellowship is the body of Christ. As such, it lives by the unity and power of his spirit. The parts that are expressed in different personalities and gifts function together under Christ's direction and in love.

The process of trust building, described earlier in the group formation stage, continues here in group maintenance. Trust is always being built as deep love grows. Our participants put it this way: "We are learning Christ's love by learning to love one another!" Self-disclosure continues. Although it is not necessarily a confession of past sins, the disclosure does parallel the confession section of a worship service. People admit "how they are." Cleansing comes with the admission of attitudes and feelings that one may bring to a gathering. Trust develops.

Sidney Jourard observes, in old-fashioned language:

> A person will disclose himself only when he believes that his audience is a man of good will. To put this another way, self-disclosure follows an attitude of love and trust. If I love someone, not only do I strive to know him, that I can devote myself more effectively to his well-being; I also display my love by letting him know me. At the same time by so doing, I permit him to love me. (Sidney M. Jourard, *The Transparent Self,* p. 4; D. Van Nostrand Co., 1964)

Loving concern in a group is more than a feeling. It is an intention, a decision that is part and parcel of the group's covenant. A promise is made to stand with others in the group. The apostle Paul suggests that we should "rejoice with those who rejoice, weep with those who weep" (Rom. 12:15), in order that we might fulfill the law of Christ (to love one's neighbor). The effect is health producing in the group.

2. *Nurture*

The small group has served long and well as a vehicle for study, but when it is confined to the study-discussion function, it tends to go stale. Head-tripping, brainstorming, and batting ideas back and forth simply reinforce one of the church's problems; namely, that we have become too cerebral! Ideas prompt chewing and tasting, but often they are not digested and assimilated.

In the basic group, study can be placed in the context of worship, fellowship, and action. These additional elements permit the base community to discover its roots in history and tradition. New communities of faith are not historical accidents. Discovery of the theological, historical, and biblical tradition provides grounding.

I recall the excitement of visiting the small fishing village in Denmark where my grandfather had lived as a child. My identity was affirmed as I soaked up the environment, visited the church where he was baptized, and fantasized about the courage and bravery of the old Vikings! The base community discovers this same kind of excitement when it walks through history, identifying with a Calvin as he attempted to build a city of faith, justice, and righteousness, or a Paul as he attempted to evangelize Corinth, or a Philemon who hosted a house church, or a sick man as he begged Jesus to heal him, or the prophet Amos as he cried out against the injustice that the rich inflicted upon the poor. God is the Lord of history, and the church lives in a stream of history. The base group finds its identity as it comes to grips with both its contemporary setting and the Christian tradition. Study and examination of the biblical and historical record becomes a must.

Study, when pursued within the context of the group's worship and mission, places the process of theologizing within the group. Too often, "doing theology" is relegated to the seminary professor or to a committee charged with the task of writing a new confession of faith. But theologizing can be a very exciting discipline for laypersons in small groups. They search for who God is, how he has worked in history, and what a contemporary affirmation of faith looks like.

3. *Worship*

The first missionary churches gathered in houses around the common meal to hear the Old Testament Scriptures, sing the psalms, read letters from traveling apostles, pray, and share the eucharist meal. In fact, the problem in the Corinthian church of gluttony and drunkenness occasioned Paul's teaching on the conduct of the Lord's Supper, which we use to this day.

The church fathers at the end of the second century described similar patterns of gathering. Justin Martyr and Tertullian record that at the table they prayed, ate as much as the hungry took, drank as much as the temperate needed, then washed their hands, lighted a lamp, read the memoirs of the apostles and writings of the prophets, listened to a discourse, sang a hymn (going to the center of the room to sing was a test to see how much the leader had drunk!), and prayed to conclude the meal. They then departed to live modestly and with chastity. Often the remaining bread and wine were shared with the poor. Their table conversations included words of encouragement, correction, or censure. The diverse gifts of many were recognized and utilized. Worship took place in the midst of a small, intense, and intimate community.

The locus for prayer/worship is threefold: *the closet, the house,* and *the sanctuary.* Each has its unique place within the disciplines of the faith. Each has its own limitations if allowed to stand alone. And each offers reinforcement when exercised in concert with the other two.

Picture them as a three-legged prayer/worship stool. Take one or two legs away, and we are left with a precarious balancing act. To overemphasize or lend more importance to one will elongate that leg. To minimize, discredit, misuse, or ignore one will shorten another leg. Either way, a tilted stool does not provide a very solid foundation on which to trust our weight.

Since the professional clergy have such visibility and stake in the Sunday sanctuary setting, we should not be surprised at which stool leg has been elongated!

Jesus practiced prayer in these three settings. He went to the desert to fast and pray: to face and go through the temptations that would compromise or negate his ministry. He left the crowds and the Twelve to find an enforced solitude. The words of the psalmist, "Be still, and know that I am God," would have been familiar to him. He taught his disciples to resist showing off with public prayers and to go to the *closet* (room), shut the door, and pray to the Father (talk intimately with Abba—

Daddy), who sees and rewards in secret. The practice of the infant church most certainly included the private disciplines of prayer. Paul's prison letters reflect the life of intercessory prayer and yearning. The early church practiced the rhythm of prayers in the desert as well as attempts to "pray without ceasing."

Jesus' prayer/worship life also extended to the *(house)* primary, face-to-face group of twelve. Their worship grew out of their experiences, feelings, and life as a community of love and trust. This corporate offering culminated in the Lord's Supper and is projected in Jesus' promise, "Where two or three are gathered together in my name, there am I in the midst."

The early chapters of the book of Acts reveal some emerging patterns for the church. "They spent their time in learning from the apostles, taking part in the fellowship, and sharing in the fellowship meals." (Acts 2:42, TEV.) For several centuries, house churches served as the locus for small groups of Christians to pray, hear Scripture, sing praise, eat meals, celebrate the Eucharist, and share offerings with the poor.

Jesus also celebrated in large crowd *(sanctuary)* settings. He taught the masses and healed their sick. He went to the synagogue ("as his custom was") and to the Temple (where he insisted that it be a house of prayer). His teaching about destroying and rebuilding the Temple did not dissuade his followers from frequenting it. Temple worship and festivals were central expressions of their Jewish faith. "The believers continued together in close fellowship and . . . met as a group in the Temple [along with other Jews], and they had their meals together in their homes." (Acts 2:44, 46, TEV.)

a. *The Uniqueness of Each Setting.* The closet, which represents the arena of *self-imposed solitude,* is a place, or a state of existence, that is free from distractions. It offers an opportunity to be alone with oneself in the presence of God.

The distinctive edge for prayer/worship in the house is the *experience of "community"* in the primary face-to-face group. The house includes those who have committed themselves to a loving and trusting community—to be the body of Christ, learn-

ing his love as they learn to love one another. It is a place for
disclosure, for confessing: telling how it is with me. It is a
community of empathy, being with one another. Gifts are recognized and called forth. Support for ministry and outreach is
maintained. Community can be a scary place as well. People live
with the paradox of having hunger for intimate community and
at the same time fearing it. The house is the place of honesty,
of teaching, of exhorting, and even rebuking. Here members are
held accountable for their lives and witness. There are few hid-
ing places. The masks are off.

If the closet is the setting for solitude prayer and the house
is the setting for communal prayer, what is left for the sanctuary? Where is its uniqueness and distinction? *Sanctuary worship
is a public recital of the drama of grace!* Certainly attention is
paid to the general experiences: the hopes, needs, aspirations of
the people. But so many people bring such a variety of moods
and needs that it would be impossible to satisfy each peculiar
one. So we rely on the great resources of tradition (that which
has been valued over the ages) and of the wider corporate
church (usually a denomination order) to move us through the
drama. The service has movement, perhaps taking its cue from
Isaiah's vision of the Lord in the Temple and his response to it.
The hymns, prayers, creeds, Scriptures, and ascriptions are not
to be the latest "cleverisms" or "cuteisms" but are to affirm the
unity of the church and the basics of the gospel of grace.

b. *The Interdependence of All.* My own experience testifies to
the need for a balanced worship/prayer life. When I give an
inordinate amount of time and energy to one, I feel a greater
hunger for the other. When they are experienced in concert, I
discover that each reinforces and lends great energy to the other.

What can the closet do for the house? It enables *community*
to be discovered as a gift, not something to be built through its
own efforts. Tilden Edwards of Shalem Institute attests to the
awareness of connectedness and community that comes in corporate silence and in following some of the common spiritual
disciplines as a small group. In fact, one of the new aspects of

group life is formation around solitude, in letting go to God, rather than through the human relations method of self-disclosure, affirmation, confrontation, and feedback. The Church of the Saviour's experience is the same. An interpersonal connectedness comes at the deeper levels of being. The closet brings the path of corporate solitude to the house.

Many small groups are moving more and more into the practice of worship, using paths of silence, solitude, and meditation. A certain self-disclosure comes at a deep level of surrender to God, not only through interpersonal sharing.

John Biersdorf reports on the experience of the Institute for Advanced Pastoral Studies:

> For us, the whole trend in small groups has been toward *worship, prayer and meditation practice.* We have found in many local churches and among clergy in our Doctor of Ministry program and other seminar programs that worship, prayer, and meditation practice *can become the basis for small-group life.* It brings the special kind of intimacy and disclosure that at the same time gives the group an operational transcendent focus, if I may use that clumsy term. That means that by building their life explicitly around the experience of prayer and meditation, they are then able both to be more intimate with each other and to work more effectively in the world. (John Biersdorf, personal correspondence, 1981. Used by permission)

Hal Edwards, who has been working with small groups for over a decade through Christian Laity of Chicago, has similar observations:

> Over the last eight years I have been deeply influenced by the outward-inward journey of the Church of the Saviour. I have discovered for myself and for others the importance of spiritual direction, silence, the psychological-theological implications taught in the framework of Morton Kelsey and Carl Jung. Over the past ten years I myself have moved more into these areas while, at the same time, I believe the relational dimension and the small-group dimension of Christian growth are very important. But I have come to discover that it is important to show

people a worldview or a framework for the unconscious and the superconscious as well as the merely conscious level of communication. (Hal Edwards, personal correspondence, 1981. Used by permission)

What does the closet bring to the sanctuary? It brings the fallow ground of *openness*. How many distractions (outer or inner) does one's mind follow in a typical corporate worship service? I would be afraid to count! But people who know how to let go, to release and center, are the ones who are in a position to hear. "He who has ears to hear, let him hear." Jesus suggests that readiness is the key to receiving. The closet frees one to give full energy to the corporate recital.

What does the house bring to the closet? It brings *identity* in aloneness (in contrast to loneliness). Faith is always personal but never private. The person in community belongs. One's identity as person is established in community (contrary to the fears of some that participation in intensive group life will blur and diffuse one's identity). The person who belongs can risk going to the inner depths of the soul.

What does the house bring to the sanctuary? It brings the laboratory of *honest life*. The house is a microcosm of the church or, as Augustine suggests, "a church within the church." The rubber hits the road first in the intensive group. Our report out from several house church consultations in the early 1970s revealed that significant issues of the larger church were first felt and identified in the house groups. The church's pain, joy, struggle, and success are immediate and visible for all to see.

The house brings the "stuff" for corporate confessions, thanksgivings, intercessions, and petitions, especially if the groups express the full marks of the church (including ministry).

What does the sanctuary bring to the closet? It brings to bear the rich tradition of the church, which becomes food for thought. Many of the meditative phrases or sayings which I attach to the rhythms of breathing come directly out of the

Scriptures (especially the psalms) and prayers of the church. The week-after-week rote recital of the liturgy often comes home to roost in the closet of personal struggle. How well I remember one woman's personal story. Broken by alcohol, unfulfilled by wealth and education, and disillusioned by marriage failure, she entered an empty Episcopal church for prayer. Suddenly the words of the old confessional prayer which she had "rehearsed" years earlier came rolling off her lips. The liturgy of the sanctuary had entered into her closet worship with purging and healing power.

What does the sanctuary bring to the house? It brings the *unity of the church.* The power and the effectiveness of the congregation are not to be found in its membership size alone, but in the number and efficiency of the living cells within it. These cellular groups will come and go—be born, flourish, and die. But like a body where cells live and die, there are some constants. There is bone structure on which the cells hang and interrelate. There is a central nervous system, which correlates command and response, pain and pleasure.

Let the congregation see itself functioning as the cathedral that gathers groups for celebrations and overall coordination. The rich diversity of groups can then function in unity.

4. Mission

I never cease to be amazed at the power of a small group that has its mind and energy wrapped around a specific mission concern. The effect is far disproportionate to the number of people involved. The mission groups (now congregations) of Washington's Church of the Saviour testify to this. From the beginning this church has insisted that groups must form around a mission call and that, without a clear mission direction, groups cannot continue to exist.

When the mission factor is present in a group, its worship has life, its fellowship is honest, and its spiritual growth is real. Too many groups postpone moving into mission until they have gotten their fellowship and worship life together. In fact, that day may never come, and the possibility is diminished by the absence of mission.

Some groups have not chosen to conduct a corporate mission in which each member is involved. They do, however, assist each member to define and be accountable to the group for his or her mission efforts. Other groups see their role as one of support for mission efforts of the congregation that are not particularly tied to a single group.

If mission is to be expressed by the group as a whole, it will generally be there at the beginning, inherent in the call. I have observed very few groups, started for the purpose of mutual support or spiritual growth, which have been able to rearrange themselves around an outreach ministry. That only happens when one or more persons get involved emotionally with some pain that lies outside the group. The transition calls for a radical shake-up of the group and a renegotiated covenant. Again the old critical issues of power, trust, and anxiety will surface.

The Pastor's Enabling Skills

1. *For Behavioral Dynamics*

The potential power of small groups in congregations can be realized only when clergy have secured adequate skills for themselves and are able to serve as trainers for the lay leaders of the groups. The pastor becomes a technician who stands by or in the ongoing maintenance functions of the group.

Decision making, conflict resolution, and intro-group communication call for good leader skills. My experience of training seminary seniors and young pastors revealed a glaring absence of the skills needed to be an enabler of small groups. Young ministers tended to be up-front, highly directive, and sanctuary-oriented. They lacked the rudimentary skills related to group formation, decision making, goal setting, evaluation, and conflict resolution. Their seminary training had centered on larger corporate gatherings or one-on-one counseling, even though much of their church leadership would take place in small-group settings. Just imagine, for instance, the hours of a lifetime that a pastor will spend assisting groups or committees making decisions!

2. *For Fellowship*

Many of the skills utilized at the group formation stage will continue to serve well for the ongoing development of fellowship. The fellowship of the group, for instance, can be deepened through storytelling. An example of the effect of storytelling in a loving group is related by R. J. Lavin, pastor of Our Savior's Lutheran Church in Tucson, Arizona:

> I have frequently referred persons to one of the Koinonia groups without telling the leaders what the problems are, but that the new members need some support as persons. . . . In one case I referred a rape victim, let's call her Mary, to a small group after I had met with her over a period of about two months with little progress in her gaining self-esteem. No matter what I said to Mary, she seemed unable to regain her feeling of dignity as a woman and as a Christian until I asked her to join a small group. I don't know how much of her story she told the group, but I do know this: she is a changed woman, completely different from the cowering woman who first told me that she was not clean. She needed and got support, love, and acceptance, which I think she never could have gotten from a counselor, at least not to the same extent she had her needs met by a Koinonia group. (R. J. Lavin, "Koinonia Groups: A Strategy for Penetration," unpublished pamphlet, p. 12. Used by permission)

One method which our own church groups have hit upon is to begin each meeting with a logging-in period (limited to 20 or 30 minutes) in which those who want can share any experiences they have had since the last gathering and any concerns, hopes, or feelings they bring to this meeting. The time limits are freeing and do keep the gatherings from bogging down to sharing and therapy sessions or from rehashing old material. At the close of each meeting they are also invited to identify what they intend to do and/or be until the next meeting. The declaration of intent creates a context for prayer and other supportive measures during the week and also helps to focus the logging-in section at the next meeting. Group members can report how their declared intention went and how they feel about it.

3. *For Nurture*

Instead of giving neat, seminary-sounding theological "answers," the pastor can assist the group to do its theology. One helpful step-by-step approach can be tied to the experience of the group or of its individual members.

Step 1. Identify an experience that has been significant and meaningful.

Step 2. Elaborate on the experience, including the feelings that were present.

Step 3. Select a symbol that best depicts the experience and the feelings.

Step 4. Connect the experience and its symbol to some aspect of tradition—Bible, history, music, art, theology. (How was it like or unlike situation X?)

Step 5. Identify any meanings, values, or learnings that grow out of the connections for you.

Step 6. State a faith affirmation that you now can make. ("I now believe that . . .")

Step 7. Declare any new intentions for the future. ("We now intend to . . .")

This experience-based model is backwards compared to our usual approach. We tend to start with our beliefs, enforce them by our values, find confirmation for them in the Bible and tradition, secure a symbol that illustrates them, and generate a behavior or experience that is desired! But the group that takes its experiences seriously and does its theological homework can discover an exciting new process of Christian nurture.

The Bible was actually written this way. The mighty acts of God were events (covenant call, exodus deliverance, wilderness wanderings, gift of land, creation of a just order) which the people of God reflected upon. They came to some conclusions about God out of their reflections, which led them to new events. Repeating the action-reflection cycle leads to growth in faith and understanding.

I asked a friend whose family had been participating in a small intergenerational faith community how his children were doing with the data of the faith. He replied: "They do not have as much exposure to the whole Bible as they would in a traditional church school class. But what they have, they really have!" They had listened to and participated in the sharing of life events along with the biblical and theological connections members of the group were making.

4. *For Worship*

The pastor whose training for and experience in worship has been in the sanctuary setting can make some helpful translations of sanctuary worship components to the house or small-group setting. Participants in one house church with which I worked struggled to identify their worship life. Their previous church experience had sent a message that *real* worship happens on Sunday, in a sanctuary, and under the control of a professional pastor. We began to identify the major components of sanctuary worship: praise, admission and release, thanksgiving, grounding in the Word and Sacrament, affirmation of faith, offering of gifts, intercessions and petitions, and a parting blessing. Then I asked them to identify what they did in house church, even though loosely structured, that was like the components of worship with which they were familiar. They were surprised that so much worship, in fact, was happening!

People engaged in new worship forms need to know why they are doing what they are doing. They should be able to relate the new to the old, the innovative to the traditional, in a conceptual framework. Examination of the old orders of worship and con-

temporary orders will reveal certain elements in common. Let's
look at a traditional order, then consider how the elements
could find expression in a small, more intimate group.

a. *The Call to Worship.* In a traditional order, the pastor
announces the call (or invitation) to worship from the pulpit. In
the small group, the members greet each other, extending words
of welcome: "This is the day which the Lord has made; let us
rejoice and be glad in it" or "The Lord is risen. . . . He is risen
indeed!" Paul gives us a clue to the lively welcome to worship
which the first house church Christians extended: he encouraged them to greet each other with a holy kiss. Come to think
of it, a hug is really a very direct call to worship. For one thing,
the leader does not get all the attention; it is passed around
within the community!

b. *Invocation.* Prayers of invocation affirm who God is and
who we are. Direct, participatory, one-word prayers can sum-
marize the affirmations and feelings of the group. Additional
methods such as silence, fantasy trips, and single-word expressions quickly bring concerns to the surface.

Prayers can be sung. Use the African spiritual "Kum Ba
Yah" (meaning "come by here"), pausing between each verse to
allow someone to articulate in one word how he or she feels. The
group can respond: "Elmer feels troubled . . . Suzie feels thank-
ful . . . Joyce feels hopeful . . . O Lord, come by here." This
acknowledges who we are and brings who we are to God.

An extended logging-in (accounting of what has happened
since the last meeting), followed by a summary prayer, gives
worship a lively start. Stress the importance of new information,
not a rehash of the old. The New Testament practice of proph-
ecy refers to reporting what God is and has been doing, as well
as foretelling what he will do in the future.

c. *Prayers.* Thanksgiving, confession, intercession, and peti-
tion are essential functions of prayer. Shared participation that
touches the "closet" concerns—the needs and dreams of people
—has vitality. Provide a relaxed or flexible framework into

which people can insert their own agenda of interests and concerns.

As a pastor I find the pastoral prayer the most frustrating aspect of worship for which to prepare. I simply don't know what is deep inside several hundred people unless there happens to be a national, community, or family event that obviously dominates their minds. Prayers I prepare on Saturday can be made obsolete by unpredictable events of the next twenty-four hours.

d. *Praise.* In addition to the use of a familiar hymnbook, there's the option of a three-ring notebook into which new hymns may be inserted. The book then becomes an account of the history of the group. Many folk hymns with easy, singable tunes are available. They can be sung without accompaniment or with guitar. Some groups buy records and sing along.

With a little practice, the group can learn "portable" responses to relate various worship activities. Multiple-use music includes the various forms of "Amen," such as the threefold amen or the "Amen" from *The Lilies of the Field;* the Kyrie Eleison ("Lord, have mercy upon us; Christ, have mercy upon us"); and trinitarian praises (the Gloria Patri or the Doxology) set to familiar tunes. Joining together as a group to write hymns can be an exciting adventure. Many psalms lend themselves to the construction of new tunes or to coupling with established tunes.

e. *Affirmation of Faith.* Traditionally we recite the Apostle's Creed or perhaps the Nicene Creed. Other historic creeds forged out of the struggle of God's people can be included in a loose-leaf binder. In addition, the group can articulate its own beliefs. Invite each person, in turn, to state in one sentence what he or she believes. (What do you believe?) Selected Scripture can also be used to affirm one's faith.

f. *The Word.* The Bible provides an unparalleled record of how God acts and who he is, as revealed in Jesus Christ. The first-century house church gathered to read the Old Testament and the circulating letters of the apostles. The Reformation made the Word central to worship. The Word was to be read and explained in language understood by the people.

Proclamation of the Word in base groups may take place as a leader teaches the Bible, as the group engages in dialogue, as participants grapple with a good book, or as the group listens to tapes recorded by preachers or teachers.

g. *The Sacraments.* During a retreat, the elements of Communion were passed from person to person, along with the instructions, "Share with each other the bread and, in your own words, the good news." When Gloria received the bread, she broke into tears. "For thirty-five years," she said, "I have participated in Communion, but it has always been another person's [the preacher's] good news." The force and power of the simple act of ministering to each other opened up the gospel in a new way to her.

Most denominations require the presence of an ordained clergyman for an authorized service of Communion or Baptism. The existence of multiple new forms of the church, however, calls for a new look at ordination and sacramental rules. For instance, if an authentic conversion takes place in a small group, why wouldn't Baptism be located there? The basic group would become the community of "God parents."

The practice of Communion in the house church can have tremendous impact. Must the clergy be present? Could church councils authorize laypersons to preside at the small-group Communion? Small groups can meet without a pastor for the purpose of Bible study, prayer, and mission planning. Could they for the Eucharist? The total church needs to look afresh at this issue. The change from the early church's common meal communion to large congregational Communion has altered not only the practice but also the *meaning* of the Sacrament. Individualism and clergy-centeredness within congregations have replaced the intimacy and corporateness of the household. John Tanburn traces the practice of the early church:

In the earliest days we know of no settled rule, even concerning the Breaking of Bread. If there was a convention in some local churches that only an elder might preside at the eucharist, it was not sufficiently important even to gain a mention in the otherwise detailed sacramental regulations sent by Paul to the chaotic church at Corinth. Clement, Bishop of Rome towards the end of the first century, wrote a long letter to the Corinthians in which he likened the apostles, presbyter/bishops and deacons to the High Priest, priests and Levites of the Old Covenant, and required members of the church to keep to their proper functions. Yet presidency at the eucharist is not mentioned. The Didache also has detailed sacramental regulations—without limiting who may offer the thanksgiving. We have to wait for the second century, after all the apostles have died, to find any limitations at all; and even then it is not restricted entirely to the local ordained minister or bishop; Ignatius, bishop of Antioch, wrote to the Christians at Smyrna, "Let that be considered a valid eucharist over which the bishop presides, or one to whom he commits it." The presbyter/bishops have not yet taken over all the ministrations of the Spirit, and some of them ruled without teaching or preaching as late as Cyprian. So far from depressing the lay body into a passive dependence on them, the ministers saw their function as "to equip God's people for work in his services" (Ephesians 4:12 NEB)—to stimulate and train them in corporate fellowship and mission. (John Tanburn, *Open House,* p. 32; London: Falcon Books, 1970)

In conclusion, what guidelines should be followed? A group may conduct love feasts or agape meals in which bread may be broken and shared without authorization or clergy presence. Regarding Communion, denomination policies should be observed. Many require the presence of the ordained clergy to officiate. Some are willing to grant permission to laypersons under limited circumstances.

h. *Offering.* Offerings include far more than what is placed in a money plate passed by boutonniered ushers. Any group can find convenient ways to collect money, but finding a ritual whereby we can offer ourselves to God and his work is more

difficult. Can we find ways to declare our intentions to the
community? *What am I willing to be and do with or for you?*
Psychologists are increasingly placing stress on the role of intentional living. The offering provides a good opportunity for intentions to be declared. Both support and accountability are practiced in the community of faith.

Place a sheet of newsprint on the floor in the center of the
group. Let individuals, couples, families, or the corporate group
write what they offer in view of everyone.

A covenant of silence can provide a setting in which each
person writes a dialogue with God on "the offering or covenant
which I make." Invite members to read about their covenant as
an act of offering (but do not insist).

   i. *Benediction.* The benediction provides a way for the group
to say good-by and to wish one another God's peace.

The ancient tradition of passing the peace suits small groups
to a T. The members clasp each other's hands, and each one, in
turn, says, "May the peace of God be with you."

The group members can huddle with hands clasped or with
arm linked in arm. With eyes open, they repeat together any one
of several familiar benedictions they have memorized. One is:

> May the Lord bless you and keep you.
> May the Lord make his face to shine
>   upon you and be gracious unto you;
> May the Lord lift up the light of
>   his countenance upon you
> And give you peace! Amen.

The song "Shalom, My Friends" can be sung while the participants shake hands, nod heads, or hug a farewell. "Shalom"
(meaning peace or well-being) may be spoken as a benediction.
Some groups borrow the "Om" practice from yoga groups.
While sitting in a circle with clasped hands or packed together
in a standing "love ball," the participants can sing "Shalom" or
hum to a loud crescendo, letting it die away slowly. People feel

the benediction as it is pronounced in humming vibrations emitted by the family of God.

Worship in the small base groups does not necessarily follow a prescribed order, although some groups may choose to do that. (The simple worship orders from the Taizé community in France are very usable.) Small-group worship is more spontaneous, more experience-reflection oriented. Participants learn to identify moments when confession, affirmation, call, and so on take place. They then can lift the moments for identification or reflection. The moments usually fit into one or more of the traditional categories of worship that have just been described.

5. *For Mission*

The pastor can assist the group to touch the pain spots in the community in hopes that a call may emerge. In addition he or she can help the group members to identify their gifts for ministry. Some good aids are available to help people locate their gifts. Ministry is the application of one's gifts to the hurts of the world. Motivation for ministry comes from the confidence of gifts and the call to stand in the arena of the world's pain.

Practice in Churches

The *functioning stage* is an appropriate place for the resources of the church to support the group. The mission budget, for instance, should be a potential source for the funds a group needs to accomplish its task of ministry. The system should be open enough to provide a way for any groups to make requests.

The official board can be organized in such a way that a particular committee or commission gives oversight to group development. This will not only provide a line of accountability but will create a feeling of legitimacy for the group. Small groups tend to fall between the administrative cracks. They have been initiated as "over and above" structures and receive little official support and have no direct line of accountability. They often become the pastor's pets; he or she becomes a personal support and accountability line. Groups can feel like orphans, while church boards often feel that a bunch of illegitimate offspring have invaded the house!

A few years ago we restudied our own church council structure in an effort to gear up to manage various aspects of our church's program and ministry, especially the small groups. The council had been organized under what I would describe as a "theological oughtness" model. We had committees for worship, outreach, Christian education, and fellowship. But from a practical standpoint our program life could not be separated out so neatly. Nurture groups practiced worship or exercised ministry. Outreach groups were engaged in study. The Sunday fellowship hour or occasional fellowship dinners were only partial occasions for mutual support and care.

For exploration, we temporarily laid aside our theological mandates and began to look at the functional lines in which the session was in contact with people. In what ways did we manage what went on?

"Manage" is often a dirty word in church circles because it connotes manipulation or cold, hard, calculating ways. But for us it became a good word. We discovered that we manage ministry with (1) individuals or their families on a one-to-one basis, (2) a whole variety of smaller groups, (3) the gathered congregation in open settings, and (4) people and structures outside the congregation. Four commissions were then formed along these functional lines and were named (1) Commission on Individual and Family Care, (2) Commission on Small Groups, (3) Commission on Congregational Functions, and (4) Commission on Extended Ministries. Each commission is to operate out of a balanced grounding in theological imperatives for the church.

Designating a commission of the official board to manage small groups has placed both support and accountability on the groups. The groups range from a softball team to a prayer group, a continuing group to a six-week seminar, and a youth fellowship group to a mission group. We have found this new approach to work well.

In an effort to keep track of groups that a committee on small groups could manage, a scroll could be devised which is an extended month-by-month flow chart. The following elements designate the progress of the group:

A call initiated by a layperson

Committee sanction and support of the call

Committee-initiated call

A time line indicating a period of exploration or evaluation

A time line indicating the duration of the group

Beginning of a covenant period

End of a covenant period

Support or consultation by the committee

Evaluation and learnings summary

Here are some examples of the small-group program of the church.

Jane Church feels the need for a support group for mothers of small children. She sounds the call to the small-group committee, which in turn affirms it and gets the word out to other potential participants. After a short period of exploration, a covenant is agreed upon for a fixed time period of ten weeks. A member of the committee meets with them during the tenth week to help them evaluate their experience and close the group.

A covenant group on nurture was called by the church officers. The contract was spelled out in the call: to meet during the Sunday church school hour for thirteen weeks to study the denomination's proposed new confession of faith. The study leader had already been recruited. An evaluation session was scheduled for the final week, conducted by representatives of the church officers.

A group was called by a layperson for the purpose of Bible study on the parables of Jesus. After two sessions the eight respondents decided to study together under shared leadership for two months. During their evaluation they spoke about what they had come to mean to each other. They then decided to continue to meet for three weeks to explore an expanded covenant, for they wanted to include worship and outreach. A member of the church staff met with them for those three weeks, during which time they formed a contract to meet as a base covenant group for two months.

A ministry focus group was initiated by a layperson who was deeply concerned for persons who were just being released from prison. A nephew who had been released had difficulty finding a job and adjusting to society. The new awareness of his plight and that of others like him gave impetus to the call. Sanction was given, and the church assisted the four persons who responded to the call to get information on prison ministries and release procedures. The covenant became very explicit, and the group (named "New Lease on Life") decided on a six-month period.

A base covenant group was initiated by a lay call for an intergenerational group of families who would attempt to experience and live all the marks of the church. The church's group life task group sanctioned it and provided a leader who helped them grow in trust and set some basic patterns. A three-person leader core from the group was trained. After six weeks of exploration they formed a covenant which was projected for a two-month period. At the time of the covenant-making, the total congregation acknowledged and prayed for them. After two months they evaluated and renegotiated the covenant, this time for three months.

6

The Terminating
Stage

> For the Lord our God shall come,
> And shall take his harvest home.
> From his field shall in that day,
> All offenses purge away;
> Give his angels charge at last
> In his fire the tares to cast,
> But the fruitful ears to store
> In his garner evermore.

I recently lifted from my journal an account of the termination of a small group that had meant much to me.

Our house church had been together for one year. Most of us had gathered as strangers. The group was intergenerational and experienced both the agony and the ecstasy of becoming a community of faith. I remember good times—when we paraphrased the psalms and set them to contemporary tunes to the accompaniment of the kids' instruments—when we built an Ebenezer at Stone Mountain and later saw it before our eyes on TV—when we went on retreat and agreed on an operating covenant—when we hosted two international visitors—when we all danced in the backyard.

I also remember the difficult times—confusing leadership patterns—concern for a family that discontinued attendance—bored children—unmet needs.

And I remember times of breakthrough—when we all really listened and cared for a person who was in a conflict situation

—when we helped pay a member's rent—when the group became a base for those in vocational and residential change—when we laughed and cried and were quiet together.

All these memories come flooding back upon me. But I remember best the last meeting—when we decided to terminate. We had gathered a week earlier after having been away from each other for part of the summer. As we each logged in what we hoped the group would be if it were to continue, one person blurted out, "I don't see that we have any basis on which to build our group." One wanted to engage in more serious discipleship, perhaps even sharing some money and material goods. One wanted to put more energy into a congregation. And another wanted to make this count as "real church." Not being prepared to make a decision, we agreed to ponder the matter for a week and return to make a "go" or "no go" decision.

Upon returning the following week, most had made up their minds to terminate the group. They said: I'm not the same person, or at the same place I was a year ago . . . I keep changing; what is good for me at one time is not necessarily good for me at another time. . . . But I really want and need the group. . . . I have in mind starting another group. It would be open to any of you. . . . I would like to terminate our contract but want to covenant to reconvene at the beckon of anyone here who wants to be surrounded with our love and care. . . . We have all become stronger (have grown up) and don't have to stay together to enjoy each other. . . . I still feel concerned and somewhat responsible to the one who wants the group to continue as is.

The decision was out in the open. We decided to "let go" and die. Many mixed feelings swirled around the room, and we knew we had to face them openly. We moved to a tight circle on the floor to create a blessing and releasing service. Our group life had been like Jacob's, an extended "wrestling" with the "angel of community." In the end we prevailed, but its "mark" had been left upon us. Like Jacob, we declared to each other, "I will not let you go until you bless me."

So we recalled and told our stories, "I remember when . . ." We laughed and wept and touched. We declared release, wishes, and prayers for each other. In the middle of the exercise someone observed, "Isn't it funny that we are really born when we have decided to die!" I expected another to respond to that statement, suggesting we reconsider the decision. But no one did. We caught the truth that life blooms when the seed dies.

And we are finished. It is done. We grieved in the open. Now we are free to gather on occasion [as we do] or not to gather. But we are not the same. The walk together was part of each person's journey in a pilgrimage of faith.

Group Theory

All groups will terminate someday. That is built into their very nature. Recognizing and preparing for this eventuality is a most critical aspect of group management.

Life-cycle understandings can be seen in the mystery of death and resurrection theology. How can something that has died continue to live? Jesus taught about losing one's life and finding it; about denying self and taking up a cross. Paul refers to the seed that dies in order to bring a plant to life. The experience of group death, when accompanied by theologizing, can provide a burst of experimental spiritual growth.

What happens near the end? What are the signs when a group begins to "fall off" from its active function? Several critical factors can be seen in various types of groups as termination time nears.

For the fellowship-style group, the critical factor is *truce*. Groups that concentrate on sharing, honesty, and growth without worship or ministry will at some point begin to plateau, then decline. The deepening trust-building process has provided energy for the group. Step-by-step self-disclosure has led to new levels of self-understanding and awareness of others. But sooner or later the group reaches its limit. To go "deeper" would become risky. To be more honest about oneself and others might inflict pain on someone else. So the group calls a truce, a gentleman's agreement. "I will not cause you discomfort or pain if you will not do so to me." The sharing group has just moved over the hill. It may not terminate immediately, but it is on its way.

Fellowship group leaders often observe that people get to the place where they can predict what any given person will say about a particular subject or event. The glow of discovery is over. Or members may have gotten all they can get from the group. Food for growth has ceased. "We've gone about as far as we can go—Truce!"

For the nurture-style group, the critical factor is *boredom.* Studies, materials, and discussion of subject matter have reached a saturation point. Members' experiences have not caught up with the information.

For the mission-style group, the critical factor is *fatigue.* People just wear out. They can only sustain a good thing so long. Sometimes their vision for the group dies, or they begin to sense a call to another type of ministry. When some people in the group begin to hear new calls, others in the group feel betrayed. Considerable energy needs to be put into group maintenance, termination, or reformation. Gordon Cosby, pastor of the Church of the Saviour, who has presided over the death of many groups, observes, "When there are no longer two or more called members in a group and this is recognized, the group may review its history, give thanks for its life, and celebrate its death" (Gordon Cosby, *Handbook for Mission Groups,* p. 64; The Potters House, 1975).

The worship-style group tends to have a much longer time span than other groups do. The ongoing process of surrender to God and the offering of prayers out of one's daily experience is a lifetime task. Perhaps the critical factors are *faithlessness, self-sufficiency,* or *sin!*

Here are some ways groups terminate:

1. *The contracted time span expires.* If the group continues, it will re-form into a new group with a new covenant.

2. *The task is accomplished.* The pastoral search committee in many congregations has become a powerful context for personal growth and group development. The committee invests deeply in the personal needs and aspirations of its members, asks

basic theological questions, deals with leadership and authority issues, has a clear-cut common purpose (to find a preacher), has the support and blessing of the larger congregation, and terminates when its task is completed.

3. *The group explodes in conflict.* If the group cannot resolve its conflict or denies that the conflict exists, it will fall apart.

4. *A covenant has not been secured.* A wide variety of expectations go unfulfilled.

5. *The group divides* or splits into two or more subgroups.

6. After a period of self-evaluation, a *conscious decision is made to terminate.* When a group is properly closed, the participants face their grief and other feelings.

7. *The leadership is not strong or matched* to the agenda of the group.

8. *The Spirit is not a bonding agent.* Common surrender to the Lord manifests itself in the gift of community at a deep level. Unity comes in a common experience of the two or three asking and agreeing in the name of Christ.

9. *Participants grow beyond what the group can offer* at their particular place on the journey.

Certain behavior patterns accompany the termination stage, often related to authority, trust, and anxiety. The group regresses back down through the dynamics of formation: power, trust, and anxiety are experienced in turn.

The final experience of Jesus with his disciples is noteworthy. The upper room gathering was loaded with emotion. That gathering pointed toward termination. Issues of power, trust, identity, and anxiety, all played themselves out. Betrayal signified distrust. Foot washing was a release of control. Arguments about who was the greatest revealed their reasserted individuality. Sleeping in the garden signified withdrawal. Peter's last-ditch effort to defend Jesus by force provided an anxious but irrational effort to save and reestablish the group. Finally, betrayal and abandonment signaled "the end" with all its residue of unfinished business.

The Pastor's Enabling Skills

As a pastor and a cultivator of small groups, I have been invited to serve as a consultant to a number of groups that were trying to decide whether or not to terminate. Their leaders were too close emotionally to the scene. The outside leader can be very helpful in guiding the members to make their own decision. Dependency patterns are heightened during closure. They need a "pastor," "consultant," and even "priest" (for last rites and funeral).

Once termination becomes a distinct possibility, the participants begin to back off, take fewer risks, and withdraw the investment of their energies.

Group termination is experienced as loss, so any of the dynamics of grief could be present: guilt, anger, denial, or depression. "The last phase, termination, would seem to be one involving dissolution of boundaries and emergence of depression and guilt. There is an attempt to win back all the deviants in an effort to create for the last time a good group." (Tim Mills, in Graham S. Gibbard et al., eds., *Analysis of Groups,* p. 173; Jossey-Bass, 1974.)

Near the termination end of the cycle, I have observed a kind of panic to get more members. At times a group may be successful in securing them, but not in grafting them onto the group's life, and termination becomes inevitable.

Within the anxieties of letting go, thanks can be offered, sins forgiven, and support granted for persons who will be taking a next step without this particular group. Often assistance is offered to help members into another group or to discern a particular new call.

The reaction to newly discovered insights of the life cycle by some pastors has been to diagnose certain groups in the congregation as dead and to plot euthanasia—mercy killing. But diagnosis and murder cannot be imposed from the outside. A skilled pastor can, however, serve a useful role as a consultant to the group that is wrestling with whether or not to let go. The leader can help people leave cleanly—without carrying unfinished business. Some steps that a leader can take to help the group are:

1. Remember and form stories about experiences and their meanings.

2. Complete any unfinished business.

3. Forgive each other and release each other from guilt growing out of unrealized goals.

4. Identify future individual growth or ministry plans.

5. Express feelings about termination. Do grief work.

6. Celebrate their life. Create symbols and rituals through which they release each other and the group to the Lord in worship.

Some of the most powerful learnings for the group will occur near the end, when everything becomes intensified. Recording these in a personal journal can cement them into one's own fabric of personal growth.

The pastor often serves as priest during the "death throes." His or her overall role as chief executive officer, manager, trainer, consultant, teacher, and pastor can make the difference for the congregation. An increasing number of pastors are now comfortable with the role of enabling the birth, growth, and death of small groups. They see themselves as priests who lift into view the symbols of hope and the traditions of life in the church.

Following the termination of Project Base Church, I recorded a description of the closing celebration which a group of skilled associates put together around understandings of the stages of grief.

It is done—but not without that strange mixture of exhilaration and pain.
I returned to Atlanta the first week of June to close out Project

Base Church. On Monday a small remnant of the 350 Skills Conference alumni gathered to sharpen their skills. Wednesday we were joined by our project associates for a learnings wrap-up. Thursday evening we were joined by friends in Atlanta area house churches for a three-hour celebration of the life cycle of the house church and of Project Base Church. By Friday it was over, so we went home.

Loren Mead had warned me that closure would be painful. I acknowledged it in my head, but during that final week it went to my gut. I was not prepared for the emotional freight, for I found myself working on a very heavy load of grief.

The Thursday evening celebration capped it off. I dreaded going into it, yet knew that was what I had to do. The celebration was planned around the stages of the life cycle of a group. We went on a pilgrimage through those stages, each of which was located at a different area of Ignatius House and hosted by liturgy teams from the conference.

On the lawn we recalled and shared our visions. In the dining hall we built trusting community. In the conference room we experienced the functional stage of worship. The chapel area was designated death and termination. For me the walk to the chapel was a via dolorosa—the way of the cross. We were led two by two into a series of rooms along the hallway. Each door was marked by one of Kübler-Ross' stages of death. In the *denial* room we talked ourselves into believing that the project was really not over. In the *anger* room I cursed death, our ultimate enemy. In the *bargaining* room we spoke of getting together again and keeping up a newsletter. The *depression* room was still and dark. The chapel became the room of *acceptance*—my holy place. I felt deeply with Bev (my partner on the way of the cross) what death and brokenness were all about. The bread and wine were their powerful symbols to me. Communion was no celebration of life. That celebration came later when we moved to the feast of the kingdom—eating and drinking with one of the most significant communities of people in my life.

Institutional euthanasia (how to terminate church programs) is a frontier which only a few are beginning to look at. I believe Project Base Church is a significant case study on that frontier. Just as a counselee gets in touch with much stuff within the last five minutes of a fifty-minute-limit session, I experienced the same in the last two months of the project. A lot of "goodies" came while I had my hand on the exit door.

I firmly believe that group termination calls for just as much sensitive attention as the formation stage! It is an area that has largely gone untouched by the social sciences. But the long and rich tradition and learnings from religious communities (as well as a theology that does not measure success by permanence, accomplishment, or longevity) leave the church as a body that is uniquely prepared to practice and reflect upon group termination.

The life-cycle concept of group life provides a comprehensive framework from which to train and support leaders. If the training period is established before the gathering of a group, the cycle can be used as a teaching tool and framework to communicate information about groups.

If the training context is within an ongoing support group of leader and practitioners, the cycle can be used to pinpoint where a group is and lead to shared reflections on specific group experiences. I always found it useful in training conferences to keep the life-cycle chart up front. It provided a handy reference map, showing initiation, formation, function, termination, and re-formation.

Practice in Churches

At the *termination stage* the linkage of a group with the larger congregation is crucial. People sometimes drop between the cracks once their group has terminated. They may need some space for being alone or noninvested, which the church can allow. They may need guidance to reinvest in a new group or to discern a call. The group itself may need to remain "dormant" for a while before it decides to re-form and agree to a new covenant.

The public worship service may also provide an important

setting for the group to let go, by announcing its termination publicly and giving thanks for its life.

This handbook has presented a comprehensive look at groups in congregations. We began with the analogy of planting seed. Perhaps that is a good way to conclude as well. For in the church we are always engaged in planting, growing, and harvesting. Termination of groups should always be seen in the shadows of new plantings and the active life of existing groups. Then the full picture will emerge.

I have felt shortchanged when I have participated in congregations that were comprised of all young families, or all older persons, or all mid-lifers. But my life has been enriched when members represented a wide variety of ages and interests. Likewise, a church that has only new group plantings or declining and dying groups does not see the full picture. A healthy blend does provide the full picture and frees people to choose in and out of groups as they are called to seek and express ministry through these groups.

Postscript:
The House Church Revisited

Our aim, we said, was to "find and feed the house church movement." This was the purpose of Project Base Church, which was launched for a three-year run in January of 1973. The project had front-end funding from the Lilly Foundation and operated under the umbrella of the Institute of Church Renewal in Atlanta, Georgia. As director of the project, I had been closely involved with the small-group and house church movement over the years. The project itself, which was ecumenical and nationwide in scope, produced some learnings that are important to the church of the 1980s and on toward the turn of the century.

Not hearing much about the house church these days, one might assume that the movement is dead. Even small groups, once the darling of the renewalists, don't get much press anymore. At the same time, if we look around, we will be surprised to see the amount of group work that is quietly going on without a lot of fanfare in congregations. Is there a "movement" afoot? Is it over? Or is it like a swinging pendulum? If so, where is it on the swing? In which direction is it going?

Perhaps these "quiet" years are a good time to go back and revisit the house church.

Since I use terminology like house church, base church, para church, intentional communities, marginal church, I should pause to insert some definition or description. By "house" or "base" I am referring to the face-to-face grouping of eight to twenty people who meet in an informal setting, usually in a home or a small, comfortable room. By "church" I mean that this group has a self-consciousness that the group is church— that it is intentional about its worship, caring, and ministry— and that it sees itself as a part of the larger church, whether formally attached to a denominational parish or congregation or informally relating to the larger Christian community through an ecumenical entity or network of other house churches.

Nothing is new under the sun. The house church was the primary structure for the church during the first several centuries of its existence. Here the Christians outloved the world. Through the pages of history, the small group accompanied renewal movements. The Wesleyan class meetings are the most notable illustration of this. Even Martin Luther originally called for the organization of house groups "to pray, to read, to baptize, to receive the sacrament, and to do other Christian works. Here one could set up a brief and neat order for baptism and the sacrament and center everything on the Word, prayer, and love." He chose rather to modernize the services in sanctuary churches "because I have not yet the people or persons for it, nor do I see many who want it." (Martin Luther, Preface, *The German Mass and Order of Service.*)

But for our purposes, I would like to chart the movement over the past several decades by five-year intervals.

1955. Ernest Southcott resurrected the term "house church" to describe what he was doing in England. Since people were not coming to the church, he took the church to the people. His book *The Parish Comes Alive* (London: A. R. Mowbray & Co., 1956) tells the story of the conduct of liturgy in the home.

At the same time in this country the Christian education programs of major denominations saw the power and potential of small groups and introduced them for discussion of information or ideas.

1960. The *serious discipleship* strand began as a reaction to the moral horror of World War II. Lay academies in Europe spawned small groups that wrestled with the serious aspect of faith commitment. Dietrich Bonhoeffer's books *The Cost of Discipleship* and *Life Together* provided heady content directions. The 1961 meeting in New Delhi of the World Council of Churches focused on "The Missionary Structure of the Congregation" and fed the structural issues to its member denominations. Notable functioning models which served to showcase the emphasis were Christ Church (United Presbyterian) in Burlington, Vermont, the East Harlem Protestant Parish in New York City, and the Church of the Saviour in Washington, D.C.

Mainline congregations that had boomed in the postwar new church expansion era began to ask, What next? Small sharing and prayer groups often were the answer. Robert Raines's *New Life in the Church* (Harper & Row, 1961) details this activity in a particular Ohio congregation.

1965. The organization of small groups within and alongside congregations proliferated. Many of these were started without the initiative or blessing of the official board or pastor of the congregation. Groups were for persons who went the extra mile. Groups were not integral to the program life of the church and felt very little accountability toward the church. Neither were congregations able to give support and resourcing to them.

This movement found strong reinforcement from para church groups which told the stories and openly encouraged group life. Faith at Work, Yokefellows, the Pittsburgh Experiment, Church Renewal, and Serendipity are the most notable. The effort was popularized through the writings of Bruce Larsen, Keith Miller, Elton Trueblood, and Lyman Coleman.

The human relations movement was just getting its start with various kinds of groups and some good learnings about small-group dynamics, but as yet they had not intersected with the church groups in any significant way.

Conference experiences, in which laypeople received a taste of interpersonal group life, also encouraged people to start a group when they returned home.

1970. Alternative forms of the church were springing up all over. In Europe these groups often found their connection to the larger Christian community through the communities that spawned and supported them: Taizé in France, the Center for Christian Unity in Germany, lay academies in Switzerland, and Iona in Scotland. In Latin and South America the *comunidades de base* (base communities) proliferated with the blessing of the church, with up-front concerns for the poor and with an experience of the Bible. The June 1973 conference at the Ecumenical Institute at Bossey on "New Forms of Communities—The Marginal Church" revealed how widespread the movement was.

In the United States denominations funded new styles of church development, many of them experimental forms for mission action, personal growth, or participatory worship. These style-centered congregations did not build church buildings and seldom grew to over forty-five members.

Several successful new church developments utilized clusters of house churches as a means of building the life and ministry in the congregation. The (United Presbyterian) Church of the Apostles in the Minneapolis–St. Paul area and Trinity (Presbyterian U.S.) in Harrisonburg, Virginia, are notable examples. Donald Allen elaborates on the Trinity experience in *Barefoot in the Church* (John Knox Press, 1972).

Who could forget the Jesus People who formed living communities of sharing and met for worship and study in small base groups? They were turned on to Jesus but turned off by the institutional church.

At the same time numerous liberated churches, unattached house churches, and Catholic underground churches were functioning. They started via reaction formation, defining themselves over against or alongside the institutional church.

At the turn of the decade two movements (both outside the church) were having a profound impact inside the church. They were the human potential movement and the charismatic renewal movement. The human potential movement made its way into church systems primarily through lay participation in sensitivity, encounter, and growth groups or conferences—and via clergy continuing education ventures into these. A great deal of theological reflection took place around such events and experiences in order to see how the learnings of the human potential movement would intersect with our understanding of the church as community, grace as unearned love, and persons as human beings in relation to God and to the world. The church was tempted to swallow the movement, along with its assumption, hook, line, and sinker, but did use restraint, as well as doing its theological homework.

Charismatic renewal also had a profound effect on the church, again with emphasis on community and spirit. (Not too far removed from the human potential movement!) Congregations found charismatic groups within their own membership or observed their members moving toward ecumenical groupings or conference settings for the immediate awareness of the presence or gifts of the Holy Spirit.

1975. By the mid-1970s the house church as an alternative structure had fallen off dramatically. When I conducted research for my book *The Base Church* in 1972 and when Project Base Church started in 1973, the movement was at its zenith. By the end of the project in 1975, most of the attention had turned to renewed hope for congregations. The 1973–1975 placement of the project provided an excellent vantage point from which to observe the movement and translate the learnings for use by the church.

We found that groups do have a life cycle and that many of the unattached groups simply fell victim to the cycle, as suggested by the Kansas study in 1971 of fifteen test groups, twelve of which were defunct two years later (see Chapter 2).

Erv Bode, a Project Base Church project associate from Grand Valley, Michigan, described the decline in the movement from his vantage point.

> In the fall of 1973, we sponsored five GVM house churches. Between 1968 and 1975, we had at various times some ten different house churches throughout the greater Grand Rapids area. . . . At this present moment, we have one house church.

... Why this great change? Why this end to the house church emphasis?

The years 1968 through 1974 were alternative years. This was due to many reasons, the greatest of them being the Vietnam conflict. People were testing new alternatives, from free schools to alternative life-styles to house churches. They were doing this for the most part outside of regular institutional structures. People interested in house churches were not finding alternative possibilities in local churches and therefore were open to new groups forming apart. We met that need in our area. . . .

But this present moment in time is the end of that alternative period! This is how I evaluate it, at least. . . . Free schools are not beginning, but mostly ending. . . . Experimental schools are not beginning, but rather are being asked to be increasingly accountable to the supporting state system. . . . Experimental ministries like ours are being asked to be more accountable to the local institutional church. . . . Part of me feels very sad about the end of this period, but I cannot ignore it and live in what is no more. (Erv Bode, personal correspondence, 1975. Used by permission)

The one remaining area for reactive formation of house churches was in feminine circles. Difficulties in the placement of female professional clergy along with the masculine orientation of the Bible and traditional liturgies sent a number of women to house churches. There they could experiment with new liturgies that would affirm their newfound identity in the church.

With renewed hope in the renewal of congregations and the apparent waning of the spontaneous group movement, attention turned to sorting out what was usable for institution building and for managing and developing the congregation.

The translation of material to insights from the human potential movement continued. A popular version of this was Lyman Coleman's Serendipity events. A theological version was Thomas Oden's *The Intensive Group Experience* (Westminster Press, 1972).

The charismatic renewal filtered into denominational group-ings. The communes of the Jesus People were breaking up. The church was taking a deep breath.

1980. By the turn of the decade an increasing number of clergy had some training and orientation in small-group process. Those who wanted to work at it in the local church would find receptivity. Most of the group work is happening in congregations that are intentional about developing their life around groups. This is particularly true in urban areas, where community via the church is one of the last remaining places to "survive." Community is seldom found in employment and neighborhood anymore.

Fuller Theological Seminary, which is the only seminary to my knowledge to offer a D. Min. in small groups, has had a full enrollment of sixty persons a year for the last five years, with a waiting list of thirty. Only pastors with five years' experience in the pastorate are eligible for the program. Roberta Hestenes, its director, observes than an increasing number who come to the program "have experience with groups," and by the end of their program, group life "is working" in their congregations.

Some cutting edges for groups in the early 1980s:

1. The small group as a setting for the practice of solitude, prayer, and meditation. Participants discover community at a deep level which has not been generated by group-building tech-niques, self-disclosure, or interpersonal relations.

2. The group as an agent for mission. This is not new to the movement, but a number of churches are now more intentional about this aspect of group functioning.

1985 (and beyond). Who knows? But the need for community will continue. House groups will develop on the "fringe" in order to pursue avenues that are closed by the institution or the culture. The economic crunch for congregations, scarce and high-priced energy, global issues, desire for simple life-style, and oversupply of clergy may continue the movement. Certainly the number of clergy with skills in group process and spiritual direction will utilize those skills in building the congregations they serve.

Index